NATURALLY

FERMENTED

Bread

First Published in 2020 by Quarry Books, an imprint of The Quarto Group, 100 Cummings Center, Suite 265-D, Beverly, MA 01915, USA.
T (978) 282-9590 F (978) 283-2742
QuartoKnows.com

Quarry Books titles are also available at diskount for retail, wholesale, promotional, and bulk purchase. For details, contact the Special Sales Manager by email at specialsales@quarto.com or by mail at The Quarto Group, Attn: Special Sales Manager, 100 Cummings Center, Suite 265-D, Beverly, MA 01915, USA.

10 9 8 7 6 5 4 3 2 1

ISBN: 978-1-63159-913-2

Digital edition published in 2020
eISBN: 978-1-63159-914-9

Library of Congress Cataloging-in-Publication Data

Names: Barker, Paul, author.
Title: Naturally fermented bread : how to use botanical starters cultivated from fruits, flowers, plants, and vegetables to bake wholesome loaves, buns, and pastries / Paul Barker.
Description: Beverly, MA : Quarry Books, an imprint of The Quarto Group, 2020. | Includes index.
Identifiers: LCCN 2020017144 | ISBN 9781631599132 | ISBN 9781631599149 (eISBN)
Subjects: LCSH: Bread. | Baking. | Fermentation. | LCGFT: Cookbooks.
Classification: LCC TX769 .B188 2020 | DDC 641.81/5--dc23
LC record available at https://lccn.loc.gov/2020017144

Design: Burge Agency
Cover Image: Joanna Good
Photography: Joanna Good

Printed in China

Disclaimer: Some plants and flowers can be poisonous and should not be ingested. Always check with a trustworthy source before using any vegetation for fermenting.

NATURALLY FERMENTED Bread

HOW TO USE YEAST WATER STARTERS TO BAKE WHOLESOME LOAVES AND SWEET FERMENTED BUNS

PAUL BARKER

QUARRY

CONTENTS

INTRODUCTION

1.
BAKING
BOTANICALLY

2.
BREADMAKING
BASICS

INTRODUCTION

YOUR BOTANICAL BAKING JOURNEY BEGINS HERE

You are about to embark on the most fascinating voyage of diskovery to bake breads and sweet buns *botanically*. Starting today, you will never have to buy yeast ever again. Instead you can just go into your garden, pick some fruit, vegetables, plants, or flowers, place them in a jar of water, and leave them in your kitchen to ferment. When the water in the jar starts to fizz, you'll then use this liquid to make your bread rise! Once this simple method is mastered, you'll be making stunning breads from just flour, salt, and fermented water. There's no need to worry if you're not much of a gardener, though; store-bought produce works just as well.

This method, which I call botanical baking (also commonly known as yeast waters), is a growing technique for baking breads. It's a natural progression from fermenting your own foods to preserve them, which continues to increase in popularity. These fermented foods are more wholesome and contain no unnecessary ingredients or preservatives. They also provide probiotic bacteria that aid digestion and increase the bioavailability of vitamins and minerals for your body to absorb, leading to healthier gut, bones, and immune system. Baking bread the botanical way will enable you to make more wholesome, nutritious, and digestible loaves. You may already be preserving your own foods at home, or perhaps you are a novice fermenter just starting out. Either way, you are about to join a clandestine group of global home bakers championing this method of baking.

As a lifelong baker who likes to push the boundaries in my craft, I have found that botanical baking is my favorite way to bake. In 2018, my botanical breads were awarded the Most Innovative Bakery Product in the United Kingdom at the national Baking Industry Awards. This was a superb endorsement for my new concept, and, personally, a wonderful accolade presented to me by my peers in British baking.

This book is a collection of my personal favorite botanical recipes, which have been developed at my bakery and training school, Cinnamon Square. The recipes all follow my *measured approach* philosophy of baking, prescribing accurate measurement of weight, temperature, and time. This helps ensure consistent quality and helps you become a more confident and knowledgeable home baker. Don't worry if you are a novice bread maker, as I am confident you will soon get the hang of botanical baking.

I hope my book inspires you to adopt this botanical approach to baking. Do share your experiences on social media and together we can champion the rise of botanical baking worldwide.

BOTANICAL BAKING

What is botanical baking? It is the method of harnessing wild yeast and bacteria abundant in fruits, vegetables, plants, and flowers to naturally leaven wholesome breads and sweet buns and further create subtle flavors and aromas.

CHAPTER 1
BAKING
BOTANICALLY

I'd like to explain baking botanically to you by first setting the scene as to where this fits in within the three existing methods of baking by using fermentation to leaven, followed by some information on fermentation itself, and finally detailing the actual botanical fermentation process. The three main categories for making yeast-raised products are bulk fermentation, prefermentation, and sourdough. I classify baking botanically as a fourth category.

AN OVERVIEW OF THE FOUR KEY BREADMAKING METHODS

1 BULK FERMENTATION

I define bulk fermentation as the "entry level" of breadmaking. Most standard baking recipes use this method, and it is the method employed within a bread machine. After a dough is formed, it is left for a period to mature. This stage is called bulk fermentation, although in many recipes, it is often referred to as the first proof or first rise. Fresh or dried yeast is used to raise the dough, and the resulting baked bread is generally completed within three to four hours. However, this process is not long enough to generate any significant natural fermentation flavor or aroma in the baked bread. In this book, bulk fermentation refers to the initial rise after the dough has been thoroughly mixed and set aside for a recommended period of time.

2 PREFERMENTATION

Once you are comfortable making bread at home using the bulk fermentation method, you can begin using the prefermentation method to step up the quality. This method requires an additional dough or batter (preferment) to be added to the recipe (e.g., flour, salt, yeast, and water) before mixing the required dough or batter. This preferment is prepared up to 24 hours prior to its inclusion within the final dough. During this time, it generates a strong fermentation flavor and aroma, and, when added as an ingredient within a fresh dough, it imparts these qualities to the finished baked bread.

There are three main types of preferment: pâte fermentée, biga, and poolish. Pâte fermentée and biga are both doughs. Pâte fermentée is a portion of a recipe that is reserved to use for the next bake, and a biga is a dough specifically made the day before to be added to the next day's recipe. Poolish is also prepared separately the day before, but it contains a higher percentage of liquid and is more like a batter. A prefermentation can also influence dough characteristics. For example, a poolish imparts extensibility, or strength, to the dough that it is used in, which is beneficial when stretching and shaping French baguettes.

3 SOURDOUGH

In my breadmaking courses, I recommend that a thorough understanding of cereal fermentation and breadmaking is attained before attempting to make a sourdough. It's not that sourdough is extremely complicated, but it does require more knowledgeable attention and craft skills to obtain the best results. As is often said, "Don't jump in the deep end before you can swim."

Sourdough is made using a sour culture to leaven the dough. Made from just flour and water, this creamy paste is left to colonize with "friendly" microbes. A mature sour culture will contain wild yeast and bacteria that produce the carbon dioxide gas to raise the dough and create unique flavors and aromas in the baked loaf. Once stable, this sour culture will last indefinitely—that is, if the correct conditions are maintained (regular feeding and stable temperature).

The sourdough breadmaking process is much slower than using commercial yeast. This allows for rich, strong flavors and aromas to develop. Other benefits from this long fermentation include making a more wholesome and digestible bread and allowing more of the nutrients present in the flour to be absorbed in the body.

BOTANICAL WATER

This refers to the newly fermented water, laden with yeast actively producing bubbles (carbon dioxide gas).

BOTANICAL CULTURE

This is a 50:50 mixture of the newly fermented botanical water and flour (generally wheat or rye) and looks visually like a 100 percent hydration sour culture.

4 BOTANICAL

As with the sourdough method of baking, botanical baking is a truly gratifying way to bake. The greater your breadmaking understanding and experiences are, the more you will appreciate just how remarkable botanical baking can be. Botanical baking will provide similar benefits to long fermented breads but with a cleaner and fresher taste.

Let's start with a brief explanation of the method and terminology you will be using in my botanical recipes. More detailed instructions on preparing and starting your botanical fermentations are provided in the section "A Step-by-Step Guide to Starting Your Botanical Fermentation."

Fruit, vegetables, plants, or flowers are placed in a fermenting jar, submerged in water, and left to naturally ferment for a few days to a few weeks (depending on which ingredient is used). Wild yeasts thriving in this newly fermented water (which I will now call *botanical water*) will raise the dough, albeit more slowly than when using fresh or dried yeast. A *botanical culture* is also made by mixing some of the active botanical water with flour (as for a sour culture, but not left long enough to become sour). This botanical culture will be used to test whether the botanical water is sufficiently active to make bread, plus it provides more active fermentation to raise the dough in which it is used.

All botanical recipes are based around four key ingredients:

Bread flour

Salt

Botanical culture

Botanical water

AN OVERVIEW OF FERMENTATION AND ITS HEALTH BENEFITS

The organisms that are responsible for fermentation are found wild in the atmosphere. Food will naturally ferment in an uncontrolled way, resulting in spoiled and inedible products (like apples that have fallen from a tree). If we can control the environment in which this fermentation takes place, we will encourage wild yeasts and friendly bacteria to thrive, leading to foods with enhanced flavors and added health benefits. This process is also a natural way to preserve foods for when not in season. This method of preserving foods has been carried out for thousands of years, but in more recent times, the craft skills necessary to preserve food have been neglected due to modern mass-production methods used to fill supermarket shelves. Fortunately, times are changing with more diskerning people realizing the lost benefits from this traditional method and the burgeoning home cooks, home bakers, and small cottage industries who champion these underutilized skills.

In this book, I focus only on starting the fermentation process and then using the fermented botanical water to raise the dough, rather than using fresh or dried yeast. Therefore, I will not go into detail about preserving foods, as there are many other books specific to this subject.

It may seem daunting, even scary, when you start off your first botanical fermentation, growing wild yeast and bacteria in a jar. Please don't be afraid. It is very easy to ferment, and if you respect storage temperatures and allow time to ferment, nothing will go wrong. Fortunately, our bodies are built with a food safety detector—our noses! If it smells bad, we instinctively know something is not quite right. If this is the case or you are just not sure, then throw it away. You have lost nothing significant, so just start again.

When baking leavened goods, we are fermenting cereals: predominantly, wheat and rye flours. Unfortunately, these cereals are rich in a phytates. These phytates are often referred to as anti-nutrients, due to the fact that they reduce the body's absorption of nutrients from the food in which they are present. Luckily, fermentation counteracts phytates and increases bioavailability. The longer the fermentation time, the less impact the phytates will have, and therefore, more nutrients will become available to our bodies. With sourdough, the reduction in pH caused by the lactic acid bacteria degrades the phytates, allowing more nutrients to become available. Other factors will influence the absorption of nutrients by our body, but this component is most relevant to our botanical baking.

Once you recognize the effect that fermentation has on phytates, it is easy to hypothesize that using additives and high levels of yeast to make bread in less than ninety minutes offers reduced nutritional value when compared to breads that have been fermented for long periods of time, like sourdough and botanical breads.

Probiotics are live strains of bacteria that, if present in the gut, aid digestion. These can be introduced through eating live yogurt or uncooked bacteria-fermented foods and drinks, such as sauerkraut, kimchi, or kombucha.

Prebiotics are substances that are found in certain types of carbohydrates (mostly fiber) that humans can't digest. The beneficial bacteria (probiotics) in your gut eat this fiber and flourish, aiding digestion. This may be why long-fermented, fiber-rich breads are found to be more digestible than modern, quickly made breads that are low in fiber.

Over the years, I've met so many customers at my bakery who have commented on their inability to tolerate mass-produced highly processed breads, yet they enjoy my breads without any signs of bloating or diskomfort. That is not a scientific study, but simply reality.

A STEP-BY-STEP GUIDE TO STARTING YOUR BOTANICAL FERMENTATION

In layman's terms, we are combining any edible fruit, vegetable, plant, or flower with water and leaving it submerged in a jar until it starts fermenting (normally for three to twenty-one days). Once fermented, the active water is used to leaven bread, buns, or laminated (layered) pastries.

1 CHOOSING YOUR INGREDIENTS TO FERMENT

Whether following the recipes in this book or selecting your own ingredients to ferment, you must first make sure they are edible; they can be past their prime, but there should be no mold or any signs of decay, such as a foul smell. If deciding on unusual ingredients to ferment, please make sure they are fit for human consumption and be aware that some harmless-looking plants and flowers are extremely poisonous. I have included a list of edible and poisonous flowers in this book (see the appendix). However, this list is not comprehensive, and you should make your own investigation as to the food safety regarding your choice of ingredient to ferment.

If you have never tried fermenting before, then I suggest that you start with apples because they are quick to ferment and can be used in many recipes.

Once you get the hang of fermenting apples, you will find fermenting other ingredients to be relatively straightforward.

Ideally, use your own homegrown produce; otherwise, search out organically grown ingredients and avoid any that have been exposed to pesticides during their growth.

Fruits generally start to ferment sooner than most vegetables, plants, or flowers due to their higher sugar content. If choosing ingredients that need some help to start fermenting, such as elderflower, instead of adding sugar in the form of honey, you could add a complementary fruit. For example, elderflower and lemon would make an ideal combination. The elderflower will supply some yeast, while the lemon will supply plenty of sugar.

After fermenting many different types of fruits, vegetables, plants, and flowers, you will probably establish a few go-to ingredients. Mine are watercress, fig and fennel, and potato and carrot.

2 PREPARING YOUR INGREDIENTS

Lightly wash your chosen ingredients to remove any soil or small insects. Yeast will be on the outer surface of your ingredients, so don't "over-clean" the ingredients. Chop the ingredients into small pieces; for example, an average-size apple should be divided into eight pieces. Cutting exposes more of the ingredient, which in turn makes the water more flavorful and releases food for the yeasts that fuel the fermentation process.

3 FILLING YOUR FERMENTATION JAR

Place the ingredients into your clean fermentation jar and fill with water, close to the top. Use a weight to submerge the ingredients just below the surface of the water to help prevent mold growth. Close the lid tightly and leave to ferment (normally, for three to twenty-one days).

A commonly used ratio for botanical fermentation is as follows:
2 parts water : 1 part botanical
ingredient(s)

This ratio can vary according to the ingredients used; for example, flower petals are very light in weight and will require more water to be added than an item such as potatoes that are dense and heavy. The most important point to remember is to use plenty of your chosen ingredient, but to make sure to leave room in the jar for an adequate amount of water, not only to completely immerse the ingredient, but also to ensure that there will be enough liquid to be used in your recipe.

When using an ingredient that is low in sugar content, such as flower petals, add 5 percent, based on botanical ingredient weight, of organic honey to the jar at the beginning. You may need to add more after a few days if there is no activity. Once you become accustomed to baking botanically, you will be able to judge how much honey to add based on your experience.

4 DAILY MAINTENANCE DURING FERMENTATION

Twice a day, stir the contents in the jar with a clean spoon. This helps release excessive gas buildup, keeps mold at bay, evens out the fermentation temperature, and stimulates the yeasts and bacteria. Also, check the temperature inside the jar daily. I like to keep it between 59°F and 68°F (15°C and 20°C). When the temperature is too low, yeast activity is slow; when the temperature is too high, mold will form on the top surface and the fermentation turns sour. If your fermentation turns sour, diskard it and start again.

You will notice bubbles appearing at the top of the liquid, and when you open the jar, you may possibly hear it sound like a glass of fizzy soda pop. When you hear this sound, you have now produced a jar of *botanical water*. This water will be used—in full or partially—as a replacement for potable water within the recipes in this book. It is also used to make a botanical culture, which is explained in the next step.

Be aware that if your fermentation is active and left unattended for a few days, your container could explode! Releasing the pressure inside, also called "burping" the container, will prevent any unwanted mess. This is a common problem when using containers with tight-fitting lids. I use Kilner-style jars with clip tops (clamp-down lids) as they "breathe" a little, preventing excessive pressure buildup.

5 HOW TO TEST IF YOUR BOTANICAL FERMENTATION IS READY FOR BAKING

By mixing equal quantities of botanical water and flour together, a *botanical culture* is made. A few hours after mixing, you should see the mixture growing and bubbling at the surface. This botanical culture is first used to check the activity of your botanical water, and then it is used again as an ingredient in each recipe for extra leavening.

HOW TO MAKE THE BOTANICAL CULTURE:

I recommend using a small 1 liter to 2 liter (2 pints to 1 quart) round lidded plastic container to mix and store your botanical culture.

To begin: Mix together 50 g (2 ounces) of flour (wheat or rye) with 50 g (2 ounces) of botanical water so they form a paste in your container, and close the lid. You now have 100 g (3½ ounces) total weight of botanical culture. Leave it to cool somewhere for 12 hours.

1st feed: After 12 hours of fermentation, add another 50 g (2 ounces) of flour and 50 g (2 ounces) of botanical water and stir to a smooth paste. You now have 200 g (7 ounces) in total weight of botanical culture. Leave it somewhere cool for another 12 hours.

2nd feed: After 12 hours of fermentation, add 100 g (3¹/₂ ounces) of flour and 100 g (3¹/₂ ounces) of botanical water and stir to a smooth paste. You now have 400 g (14 ounces) total weight of botanical culture. Leave it at room temperature to ferment for approximately 4 to 6 hours to double in size before using it in a dough recipe.

This example makes 400 g (14 ounces) of botanical culture. Using simple math, you can adjust the weight of flour and botanical water used in the initial paste to produce a second feed total weight of your choice.

6 READY FOR BAKING

Once you have active botanical water and botanical culture, you are ready to botanically bake. I recommend using these as soon as possible to obtain maximum fermentation and the cleanest flavor and aroma in your bakes.

7 HOW TO KEEP YOUR BOTANICAL FERMENTATION FRESH

Once active, your botanical water will be suitable to make breads for a couple of weeks. After that time, the botanical water will gradually reduce in activity (become less bubbly). If that happens, I recommend adding some honey, which quickly rejuvenates the combination and adds a few more days' usage.

I have found using a wine fridge is ideal for longer storage of active fermenting jars as the temperature inside can be set for approximately 61°F to 64°F (16°C to 18°C). When you want to use this botanical ferment, you can bring it back to room temperature for a couple of days to increase its activity.

Alternatively, if you store your active fermenting jar in the refrigerator at 36°F (2°C), it will stay fresh for even longer. Again, the jar needs to be brought back to room temperature for it to be fully active. Also, this ferment may well benefit from a spoonful of honey or by adding more of the ingredient that is being fermented.

Another way you can keep the same ferment longer is to replace the entire fermented ingredients with a fresh quantity, but to reuse the old fermented water. A day or two later, it will be fizzing and smelling fresh.

Aim to keep your ferments for around three weeks as it is so quick and easy to make a fresh batch. To ensure you never run out, start a fresh batch three to seven days before you intend to dispose of your existing botanical ferment.

IMPORTANT EQUIPMENT FOR FERMENTING AND BAKING BOTANICALLY

If you already bake bread, then you may not need much more equipment to bake botanically. Ideally, your home baker's tool box would contain all the necessary equipment, such as a stand mixer with dough hook (or your hands!), plastic weighing and mixing bowls, digital weighing scales (in grams), bench and bowl scrapers, food-grade lidded plastic containers for proving, proving baskets, timers, tea towels, baking paper, heavy baking trays, baking stone, lame, serrated tomato knife, baker's peel (pizza peel), and of course, a good baking oven. Other equipment you will need specifically for the botanical fermentation include the following:

FERMENTING JAR

The most important piece of extra equipment you will need is fermenting jar. I recommend a Kilner or Mason jar to start. It is possible to use a 2 liter (2 quart) plastic soda bottle with a screw cap. I find these a bit difficult to fill, whereas the jars are much easier due to their wider openings. Some jars, generally the larger ones, are available with a dispensing tap close to the bottom. This is useful as any sediment is left behind when the fermenting water is dispensed. You will need to release the top lid before opening the tap; otherwise, the liquid will not flow out. Note that if you have a lot of sediment and seeds at the bottom of the jar, these will annoyingly block the dispensing tap when trying to release some botanical water.

Some jars have a weight that fits neatly inside to keep the ingredients submerged. This helps prevent mold from forming on any part of the ingredient protruding from the water.

You can make your own weight by using a small saucer that fits snuggly inside your fermenting jar and setting a small weight on top of the plate. You normally can find something in your cupboard that will suffice, such as a small ceramic or glass ramekin, but make sure to avoid metals as these may react in the water.

THERMOMETER

This tool is important for maintaining your fermenting jars within an optimum environment. Store your jars in a cool location away from direct sunlight. I recommend storing them at 64°F to 71.5°F (18°C to 22°C) to achieve a steady, more controllable buildup of fermentation.

A digital thermometer is ideal for regular checking. Stir the contents of the jar while checking the temperature to even out any variations inside the jar; stirring also can increase the activity of the fermentation.

You can apply a stick-on thermometer (as used on aquariums) to the fermenting jar. Using one of these, you will be able to see what the current temperature is at a glance.

STRAINER

When your botanical water is ready to use, you will need to pour the water from the top through a strainer, unless you have a dispensing tap. I would recommend using a fine-mesh strainer to trap any pits, seeds, or sediment.

THE IMPORTANCE OF HYGIENE

For a successful botanical fermentation, it is important you start with clean equipment and that you work in a hygienic manner. This will ensure that your botanical fermentation starts off in a sterile environment, which will help guarantee fruitful results.

Clean all equipment, including the fermenting jar, in hot soapy water and then thoroughly rinse in very hot water and let air-dry.

When preparing your ingredients for fermenting, wash off any dirt and bugs. Be mindful that you do not want to "over-clean" your ingredients as you will remove all the yeasts from the surface. Use clean, sanitized hands or wear disposable gloves when cutting ingredients. Use a clean, dry cutting board and a sterile knife.

Fermenting botanical ingredients and sour cultures attracts fruit flies. I'm at a loss as to where they appear from; they just turn up uninvited. My advice is to keep the outside of your jars clean, especially around the lid.

There are different methods for keeping fruit flies at bay. You can buy fruit fly traps at the store or make them yourself. To do so, place some of your fermenting liquid in a small cup and add a few drops of dishwashing liquid. The dishwashing liquid will reduce the surface tension of the water, so when the flies are attracted to the smell of your ferment, they will drown in the water. This method works to catch some but not all of them. A few may still annoyingly hover around your fermenting jar!

I recommend setting up something to catch the flies before they start to appear. This will help prevent an unwelcome accumulation of them. Please note it is generally not a sign of poor hygiene when they appear. I personally think these little creatures have great taste, as they absolutely love my Belgian chocolate ganache!

KEY INGREDIENTS FOR BAKING BOTANICALLY

There are minimal required ingredients for botanical breadmaking, but each ingredient plays a vital role in the process. Therefore, it is important to source top-quality ingredients and weigh them precisely.

FLOUR

This is the main bulk ingredient and provides the structure of baked bread. Around 60 percent of a standard loaf will be made up of flour.

Flour provides the gluten network required to hold on to the carbon dioxide gas produced by the yeast, which enables dough to inflate. Try to imagine millions of tiny balloons inside your dough expanding from the pressure of the gas building up.

Flour provides strength to your dough, which maximizes the tolerance required for the shaping, proving, cutting, and baking stages.

SALT

Salt imparts flavor to your bread.

Only a small amount of salt is used (normally 1.5 to 2 percent of total flour weight). Precise weighing is vital to obtain the correct amount because salt kills yeast. When dispersed within a dough, salt controls yeast activity by preventing it from becoming too wild. Over-weighing salt will hinder the yeast from producing carbon dioxide gas, preventing the dough from rising. Conversely, under-weighing salt will produce a "wildly" fermenting soft and sticky dough with no tolerance for the remaining process.

Salt strengthens the dough to provide increased tolerance required during the shaping, proving, cutting, and baking periods.

BOTANICAL WATER

The botanical water, or water from our ferment, is mixed with flour and salt to form the dough for botanical bread, buns, and pastries. It provides necessary yeasts and bacteria for fermentation within the dough. It also imparts flavor and aroma to the baked bread. The strength of these qualities is determined by the type of ingredients fermented and the quantity of the botanical water used in the dough.

The amount of total botanical water used in a recipe will influence the rate of fermentation. As a guide, if you are fermenting ingredients low in sugars, such as flower petals, then all water in the recipe should be botanical. When ingredients high in sugar, such as tomatoes, are fermented, a more powerful botanical water is achieved and therefore less is called for in the recipe. Tap water is used to replace the amount removed. Reducing the amount of botanical water will also decrease the flavor intensity. Once accustomed to working with botanical ferments, you will be able to judge how much of the recipe water should be botanical and how much should be tap water.

BOTANICAL CULTURE

The botanical culture is a paste made from equal quantities of flour and botanical water (similar in consistency to a 100 percent hydration sour culture). It is used as a quality-control check, to establish if the botanical water has enough activity to leaven a dough. The botanical culture provides extra yeasts and bacteria for dough fermentation and imparts additional flavor and aroma to the baked bread, buns, and pastries.

OTHER INGREDIENTS USED IN BREADS

Additional ingredients can be added to improve shelf life, to add texture and flavor, and to enhance the visual appearance.

Fats such as white vegetable shortening, oil, and butter are added to provide softness to the bread—especially buns—which helps keep the products tender for longer periods.

Dried fruits, nuts, and seeds are added for texture and taste and are perfect for complementing the flavor of the chosen botanical ferment. They also add visual attractiveness, especially when you cut through a baked loaf.

EXTRA INGREDIENTS FOR BOTANICAL SWEET BUNS

When making sweet fermented buns, the cooking method and core of the recipe are still rooted in basic bread ingredients: flour, salt, yeast, and water. Other ingredients, mainly eggs, butter (or other fats), sugar, and milk are then added, some at relatively high levels, to transform the mixture into sweet and tender products.

VARIETIES OF BREADMAKING FLOURS

If you consider that roughly two-thirds of a loaf of bread will be flour, you'll see it is vital that the flour is fit for its purpose.

Using the correct breadmaking flour will provide the required strength and tolerance to the dough made from it. The gluten network developed in the dough from kneading will hold on to the carbon dioxide gas produced by the yeast, trapping the air bubbles within. As the resultant dough expands and then bakes, the internal structure sets to an edible crumb encased within a rich, flavorful, caramelized crust.

There are many flour types and strengths available, and all of them have their breadmaking suitability influenced by the strain of wheat and the environmental conditions during the growth of the wheat.

I recommend you use strong breadmaking flours for the recipes in this book. However, my "strong" flour will inevitably differ from the flour you may purchase. Therefore, whenever you try a recipe from this book, or any other source, you may need to "tweak" it slightly. Most of the tweaking will be the adjustment of water content or possibly an extra reshaping during bulk fermentation to build more strength to the dough. These adjustments may not be huge, but if you are pleased with the final result, it is worthwhile to note the difference in the ratios for the next time you use the same flour.

Much of the wheat flour we use today is classified as *modern* wheat. For years, these strains of wheat have been manipulated by man for many reasons, including improving their breadmaking suitability, producing higher yields, reducing cost, and making them pest- and climate-resistant. Modern wheat has also been blamed by some for the rising claims of wheat intolerance. This has led to the increased use of *ancient* wheats and grains, as these are unadulterated and offer more flavor, fiber, vitamins, and minerals. Ingredients like amaranth, buckwheat, einkorn, farro, freekeh, khorasan (kamut), millet, quinoa, sorghum, spelt, and teff are commonplace in breadmaking.

It is common practice to blend the ancient grains with a wheat flour, as the ancient grains are usually less suited for breadmaking; some of them contain no gluten at all. You can replace the wheat flour with your choice of ancient grain, weight-for-weight, in most bread recipes. I recommend starting at lower levels of 10 to 20 percent of the grain weight and note any changes to the water absorption, dough handling, and dough tolerance. Make any necessary adjustments for the next bake and increase the level if you feel comfortable.

WHY THE AUTOLYSE TECHNIQUE IS USED IN BREADMAKING

The *autolyse technique* is the practice of presoaking flour and water for a period of time *before* adding the salt and mixing until the dough is fully developed. Benefits include the following:

The added time allows the flour to absorb more water without competition from the salt.

There is improved gluten formation due to the increased water absorption.

This method increases extensibility to the dough, which improves dough handling and allows for increased expansion in the oven.

It allows for the development of maximum gluten from weaker flours and higher hydration doughs.

It reduces the mixing time and effort required to fully develop a dough.

If your recipe does not call for a period of autolyse, you can still incorporate this technique.

To begin the autolyse process, stir together the flour and water portions of a bread recipe—keeping back 50 g (2 ounces) of water to use to dissolve the salt—and allow this mixture to stand for 30 to 60 minutes; it sometimes can take longer, especially if you are using a stone-ground whole wheat flour that benefits from a longer autolyse time. After this period of autolyse, add the salted water and any remaining ingredients and mix until a developed dough forms. The remaining process stays the same.

The botanical culture and botanical water will be part of the autolyze process.

Some recipes in this book will give you the option to use increased water levels to produce higher hydration doughs. When using these higher-hydration dough recipes, I recommend you incorporate a period of autolyse. During the subsequent bulk fermentation period, you may need to give extra reshaping or use the slap-and-fold method (see page 34) to build more strength in the dough, as wetter doughs are slacker. Dough that is normally proved on trays will need to be proved in bannetons (proving baskets) instead to prevent spreading. The proved dough pieces will benefit from a period of retarding, enabling you to successfully turn them out of the bannetons and score them prior to baking.

I would only recommend making high-hydration doughs once you have a sound understanding of breadmaking theory and have attained good craft skills.

BOTANICAL BAKING ALLOWS FOR EXPERIMENTATION

Once you have mastered making botanical fermentations and subsequently made delicious bakes from them, you should have the confidence and experience to experiment. Botanical baking allows you to create wonderful combinations of flavors and aromas in your bakes. All you need to do is pick the recipe in this book that makes a style of bread you enjoy and then change the ingredients that are used to start the botanical fermentation.

You can plan and create your own flavor combinations by thinking about what currently is or soon will be in season. Or consider ingredients you would like to try to ferment to develop flavor combinations special to you.

It is rewarding to ferment your own homegrown produce or to use ingredients grown by family and friends. I'm sure they would be thrilled to see their homegrown produce transformed into some wonderfully baked breads, buns, or pastries. Botanical baking is a great enrichment to a self-sufficient lifestyle. You may even find yourself growing things in your garden specifically to include in your daily loaf!

Consider additions to the dough such as herbs, spices, seeds, dried fruits, nuts, or cheeses, all of which can be added to impart complementary flavors, visual intrigue, and textural differences.

CHAPTER 2
BREAD MAKING
BASICS

Flour, salt, water—that's as basic as it gets! The magic of bread making comes from understanding how to combine these ingredients to create fermentation, plus how to develop the most wonderful flavors, aromas, and textures.

Bread making experience is invaluable but takes time to acquire. Baking regularly and experimenting with different techniques will build your experience and install confidence. Don't worry if you have a bad bake—we've all had them. But try to establish what went wrong, as this will add to your knowledge base.

Passion is the unseen ingredient of great bread. Passion comes from within; therefore, I hope the recipes, tips, and techniques in this book inspire you and release a desire to make naturally fermented bread.

In this chapter I share my most useful tips and techniques for your guidance and for providing consistency to your bakes.

WEIGHING IN

Did you know that a cup of flour weighed from the top of a flour bag will be lighter in grams than a cup of flour from the bottom of the flour bag? This is because the flour at the bottom of the bag is more compacted, and therefore, you will have more grains in the same amount of space. Because of this, using a measuring cup rather than weighing in grams can cause significant variation in the consistency of your bakes.

RECIPE ADVICE AND STRUCTURE

I write recipes in a structured way, enabling you to confidently reproduce them. Do make sure to read through them a couple of times before starting. I find it helps to feel more organized.

I advocate the use of weighing ingredients in grams, including liquids, as this enables greater accuracy and improves consistency in your baking. I have included ounce equivalents if you have not yet converted to grams. Using digital weighing scales eliminate errors in your preparation. Always weigh your ingredients in separate bowls before starting, as some may require conditioning before use.

Allow enough time to obtain and ferment the required botanical ingredients for your chosen recipe. Some botanical ingredients may take two to three weeks to become fully active.

Most of the recipes will indicate the water percentage used against the weight of flour. I have included this for the advanced bakers who like to know the hydration level of their dough. This is known as *baker's percentages*, which compare all individual recipe ingredients against the weight of the *total* flour. (If more than one flour is used in a recipe, then the total weight of both flours will be expressed as 100 percent.)

A basic bread recipe would be as follows:

Bread Flour	100 percent	600 g (1 pound 5¼ ounces)
Salt	2 percent	12 g (½ ounce)
Yeast	2 percent	12 g (½ ounce)
Water	65 percent	390 g (13¾ ounces)

This gives a total flour hydration of 65 percent.

A *botanical* recipe would be as follows:

Bread Flour	100 percent	500 g (1 pound 5¼ ounces)
Salt	2 percent	10 g (⅓ ounce)
Botanical Culture	40 percent	200 g (7 ounces)
Botanical Water	66 percent	330 g (11½ ounces)

As the botanical culture consists of 100 g (3½ ounces) of flour and 100 g (3½ ounces) of botanical water, the total recipe flour increases to 600 g (1 pound 5¼ ounces) and the total botanical water increases to 430 g (15 ounces).

This gives a total flour hydration of 71.6 percent.

For your convenience, I have included an optional water level increase guide to enable you to change the main recipe into one that will produce a softer (higher-hydration) dough. This guide is for the benefit of the more experienced home baker, as many have a preference for which level of dough hydration they commonly use.

Naturally fermented doughs take a long lime to prove, or proof, before baking. You will need to gauge how fast your dough is proving and allow 1 hour before it is fully proved to preheat your oven to a temperature hot enough for baking. Please consider the proving times stated in my recipes as a guide only. Botanical breads generally prove at room temperature for 2 to 4 hours before baking, but if the conditions are not optimal, then they may take a few extra hours. Botanical buns, however, take much longer to prove, mainly due to the high sugar content. These can take up to 6 hours if conditions are perfect, but don't be afraid to let them prove for 24 hours at room temperature.

KEEPING TIME

Sometimes, just one timer may not be enough!

It may seem a bit over the top, but when you are baking, you may have four or five things on the go at any one time.

My advice is to write down next to each timer which task it is set for so you won't lose track of what you are doing.

The photograph opposite is what I use at Cinnamon Square for my oven, which has five separate chambers.

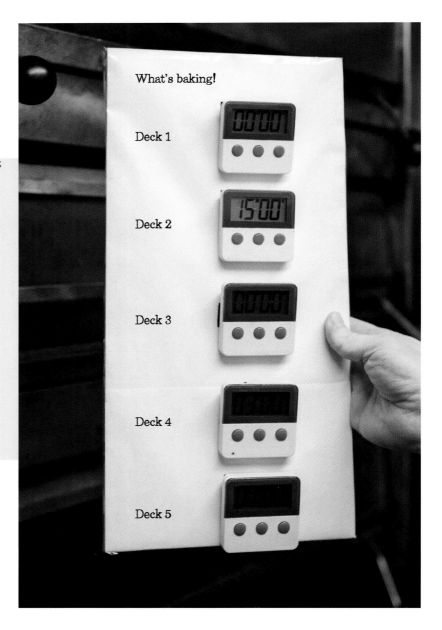

CORRECT WATER TEMPERATURE FOR BREAD DOUGH

Many recipes say to use tepid or cold water to make bread. My advice is *never to use cold water*. Yeast produces carbon dioxide gas in the dough that in turn raises it. This process only happens if it is nice and warm. The colder the yeast becomes, the less active it will be. That is why you can place dough in the refrigerator overnight and it does not grow. If you use cold water in your dough, the yeast will be less active, and if your recipe states to leave it to prove for 1 hour before baking, it will be under-proved and too small to be baked. An experienced baker would know to leave it longer before baking, but if you are following that recipe precisely, then you may well have made the dreaded "brick."

You should always, as a minimum, use tepid water, or, if your room is cold, make it a little warmer. I aim to have my bread doughs at 77°F (25°C). This is an ideal temperature to make a nice calm, steady dough. If the dough is warmer, it proves too fast, so remember my motto: *real bread takes time.*

There is an actual formula to work out the correct water temperature to achieve a desired dough temperature:

> Twice Desired Dough Temperature – (minus) Flour Temperature = Water Temperature

Assuming I have tested my flour temperature with a thermometer, and it reads 68°F (20°C), the formula would be as follows:

> 2 x 77°F = 154°F - 68°F = 86°F
> or
> 2 x 25°C = 50°C - 20°C = 30°C

Therefore, to achieve a dough temperature of 77°F (25°C), I would need to warm the water to 86°F (30°C).

Using this formula to achieve the optimum water temperature will improve the consistency of the breads made from it. Please note that room temperature, equipment, and work surfaces will influence the dough temperature too.

THE SLAP-AND-FOLD METHOD OF KNEADING

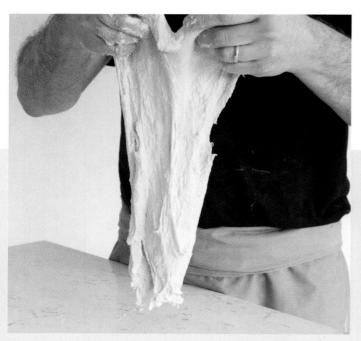
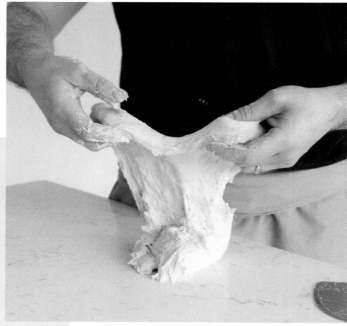

Kneading a wet dough requires a different technique than that of a typical firmer bread dough. When the ingredients have been combined, turn out the wet mixture onto the table and knead until smooth and elastic, using the *slap-and-fold method*, which is very different from the traditional kneading method.

To begin the slap-and-fold method, hold the dough in the air so that it is hanging downward. While continuing to hold the dough, slap the bottom half against the work surface and then stretch and fold the remaining dough that you are holding over the top of the dough that is touching the table. Immediately pick up the dough with both hands from the left or right end and let it hang downward. Repeat the slapping and stretching action. After a few attempts, you will find a good rhythm. Now, keep this going for at least 10 minutes. The quicker you can keep a rhythm going, the less chance it will stick to the table.

Use the windowpane test (see page 36) to check if the dough is fully developed. This dough should stretch way more than a bulk fermented split tin loaf dough.

THE WINDOWPANE TEST

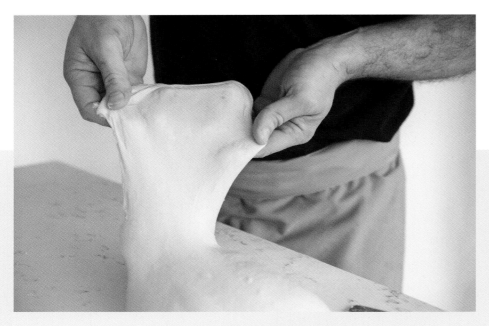

You are ready to test whether a dough is fully kneaded after you start to notice that the dough has become smoother and more elastic, and less tearing occurs as you knead. The windowpane test is your final quality control test. Take a small piece of dough, roll it into a ball, and leave it to rest for a minute. Next, flatten the ball between your fingers and gently stretch the dough until you can see your fingers through it without the dough tearing (like a balloon expanded to the maximum). If the dough stretches well without tearing, you've reached a good level of gluten development—the dough is thoroughly kneaded and ready for the next step of the process.

RETARDING (OVERNIGHT REFRIGERATION)

Placing dough in the refrigerator for an extended period offers some interesting benefits: increased flavor, aroma, and crust color, in addition to some flexibility as to when you bake your loaf. It also makes scoring your dough much easier, especially when scoring high-hydration doughs.

There are many ways retarding can be carried out, but I will focus mainly on just one method for these recipes.

When making breads from the recipes in this book, you can interrupt the proving stage and place the shaped dough into the fridge. The cold temperature of the fridge will minimize further dough expansion, allowing you to bake the dough at your convenience. You can also make larger size doughs to make enough bread to last you a week. By retarding the individual dough pieces, you can bake one loaf every day. You should notice a reduction in oven spring, increased color, and stronger sour flavor over the period of a week.

The following rules should be observed for retarding to work successfully:

Your refrigerator must be capable of holding a temperature of 36°F (2°C); otherwise, if it runs warmer, the dough will keep expanding and feasibly over-prove while out of sight.

Place the shaped dough pieces into the refrigerator at three-quarter proof of what you are aiming for. This will allow for some dough expansion while it is cooling down and during storage. If you have never retarded dough before, you may need a few attempts to find the correct level of proof before placing the dough pieces into the fridge. Take some photographs as reference for future bakes.

Cover the dough pieces in plastic or place them into lidded plastic containers while in the refrigerator to prevent drying (skinning) of the dough surface and stop any absorption of strong flavors from other items that may be sharing the same shelf.

Score and bake directly from the refrigerator. As the dough will be proved, there is no requirement for it to come to room temperature before placing it into the oven to bake.

I have kept dough in the fridge for eight days and still baked a decent loaf from it. However, the gluten structure within the dough will start to weaken and "sit back" (start to gradually collapse) the longer it is in the fridge. The length it can stay in the fridge is determined by many factors, including the temperature of your fridge, fermentation activity of the dough, length of fermentation before placing it in the fridge, degree of gluten development, and dough temperature.

HOW TO MAKE YOUR OWN PROVING BOX

This may appear simple, but believe me, it works perfectly. You don't need a special proving drawer inside your oven; all you require is a deep, lidded food-grade plastic storage box to prove your dough. Place your pans or tray inside, put on the lid, and leave the dough to prove. If it needs a little warming up, place a cup with some boiling water inside. This will provide a little warmth and humidity inside the storage box. You can remove the cup if it gets too warm or wet. I use these plastic storage boxes for most of my proving requirements at Cinnamon Square, even though I do have an industrial proving cabinet.

HOW TO TEST WHETHER A DOUGH IS FULLY PROVED

It is important that dough is fully proved before being baked. Under-proved dough will burst violently in the oven and the crumb structure will be tight. Over-proved dough can collapse, look sad, have poor crumb structure, and lack color in the oven. So, it is essential to place the proving dough in the oven at the correct stage to ensure the best opportunity for the perfect loaf. How can we tell when the dough has reached full proof?

It's relatively easy if you bake in a loaf pan. By placing the same quantity of dough in the same size pan every time, you will be able to judge when it is ready for baking just by looking at the height of the dough (once you have determined what the optimum fully proved height is). This is the same when using proving baskets.

If you prove dough on flat trays, you will need to feel the dough at intervals during proof. At the onset of proving, the dough will be dense, and when pressed with your index finger, it will feel firm. As the dough expands, it begins to feel less firm. When it reaches a fully proved condition, the indent left from pressing your index finger into the dough will stay there, and you will notice the dough beginning to feel weak.

If you plan to score the bread, it is important to know that some styles of scoring require the dough to be slightly under-proved in order to accentuate the shaping of the cuts and produce the classic bursting *ear* or *eyebrow* effect.

Consistently judging the perfect proof comes with experience. Don't be disheartened if you get it wrong. You will learn from it and still have homemade fresh bread for your troubles.

WAYS TO SCORE DOUGH

Most fermented doughs are cut with a knife directly before they are placed in the oven to bake. This cutting not only decorates the bread and makes it more attractive when baked, but it also allows for the final expansion in the early stages of baking to occur in a controlled manner. Cutting of proved dough does require skill, which will come from experience. Unfortunately, there is really nothing else other than proved dough on which to practice; therefore, you will need to make bread regularly to attain these skills, *and there's nothing wrong with making bread regularly at home!*

I use three different knives for my scoring. Each one has a specific use. Whatever knife you use, make sure it is sharp. This ensures the cleanest cut is achieved and minimal damage is caused to the proved dough while scoring. All knives will lose their sharpness, so it is important that you replace your knives regularly.

TOMATO PARING KNIFE

This is my favorite all-around bakery knife, ideal for scoring straight lines on proved dough—a split tin loaf or bloomer bread, for example. This serrated knife works so well because the serrations are small and close together, making this knife extremely sharp.

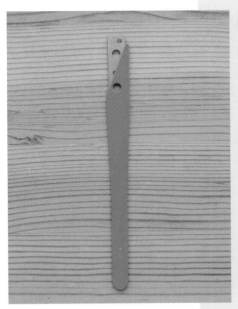

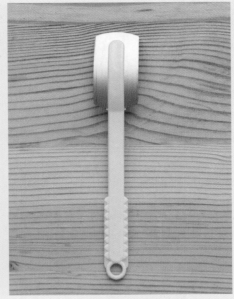

STRAIGHT DECORATIVE BLADE

Some breads can be decorated all over to create patterns and images such as stalks of wheat or flowers. For this you need to lightly score this pattern on the proved dough. With so many shallow cuts, the proved dough will gently expand in the oven, retaining the delicate design. You can purchase disposable plastic-handled blades for intricate scoring of proved dough or you can use a razor blade on its own. You will need a steady hand, good eyes, and a predetermined design.

CURVED LAME (GRIGNETTE)

This tool utilizes the fineness and sharpness of a razor blade placed in a curved position. Using this knife makes it possible to achieve the classic bulging ear or eyebrow famous on a baguette but commonly seen on sourdough breads too. Scoring the dough when only three-quarters proved accentuates the bulging effect. These blades blunt very quickly, so change them regularly. You can turn the blade around to use the other side. Because only the top third of the blade is used to score the proved dough, it is possible to use the blade, until it blunts, four times. You can buy some blades that have each corner numbered. Alternatively, you can mark the corners of each new blade before use.

You can purchase lightweight plastic handles to hold the blade in a curved position or you can use a wooden coffee stirrer stick and insert the stick through one end of the middle of the blade and then out through the other end. This will naturally curve the blade. A word of warning: Be careful with the sharp edges when removing and inserting new blades.

ADVICE ON GAS, ELECTRIC, AND CONVECTION OVENS

So, which oven is the best?

If your oven works and holds the set temperature, that is ideal. Always keep a baking stone inside your oven ready to use and you should get some great results with the recipes in this book.

Gas ovens are very good to heat a chamber, plus they produce moisture during the bake, which can be beneficial to many products. When baking bread, I often moisten the oven by pouring some water into a hot roasting pan in the oven, which immediately produces an abundance of steam. Creating too much instant steam can blow out the flame. I have a gas Aga oven at home, and this produces some lovely bakes.

I find electric ovens more controllable, especially if you have independent top and bottom heat supplies. This feature "fine-tunes" the bake to help prevent over baking of the top of a product, while still providing a strong heat source at the base.

In my baking courses, I guarantee one of my guests will ask my advice about convection ovens (with a fan) verses static ovens (without a fan). My response is normally along the lines of . . .

"My preference will be to use a static electric oven for baking and a convection oven for roasting meats and vegetables; therefore, static for bakers and convection for chefs. Most bakery products rise in the oven. Some only increase a small amount, such as biscuits, but some rise significantly, such as breads, sweet fermented buns, and laminated pastries. This rising takes place from the onset of baking and generally stops by the midway point (approximately); from then on, a skin has formed, preventing further rise. This skin then darkens and thickens, forming the crust as it caramelizes toward the end of the bake time. When the same product is baked inside a convection oven, it is exposed to a torrent of heat passing over the exposed top surface from the onset. This accelerates skin/ crust formation, which therefore restricts the potential growth of the product being baked. As there may still be carbon dioxide and steam being produced inside, the product can burst wildly out of the weakest point (often the sides), form sloping tops (especially on cakes), or have an unexpected strange appearance. Some convection ovens will allow for the fan feature to be turned off, creating a static oven. If this option is available on your oven, then try all future baking with the fan off, and when roasting meats or vegetables, turn it back on."

With whichever oven you use for baking, always allow enough time for your oven and baking stone to thoroughly heat up when planning to make your recipes. In this book, I make no reference to preheating your oven in each of the recipes, as it should be the first thing you think of when deciding to bake.

HOW TO CREATE STEAM IN THE OVEN

Creating steam in the oven at the onset of baking bread allows the dough to fully expand before the setting of the crust, thus you achieve maximum height in your bread. It also produces a crispier and shiny crust. Place a roasting pan on the bottom of the oven and allow it to get very hot. Place your dough into the oven, immediately pour some water (try 30 g [1 ounce]) into the roasting pan to create a generous amount of steam, and then close the oven door to trap the steam. The dough rises and sets in the first few minutes of baking, so don't delay in creating the steam. If you have a gas oven, be careful, as too much steam will blow out the gas; I found out that piece of information too late in my Aga oven at home!

After 15 minutes of baking, I recommend releasing the steam by opening the oven door slightly—*note that this will be very hot, so keep your face well away as the steam releases.* When all the steam has dissipated, close the oven door and continue the baking in a dry oven to encourage a crispier crust formation.

HOW TO BAKE OVEN BOTTOM BREAD

Baking on the bottom of the oven in a bakery produces breads with exceptional crust. To recreate this in your own home oven, you can use a pizza baking stone or an upturned heavy metal tray. Both must be preheated before placing the dough on top to bake. Gently place the fully proved dough onto the baking stone using a pizza peel or a couple of spatulas. Alternatively, if using an upturned tray, slide the dough and the baking paper underneath, to prevent sticking, onto the upturned tray.

The heat from the stone or tray penetrates the dough quicker and imparts a greater rise and crispier crust. Even if you are baking bread in a loaf pan, I always recommend placing the pan on a hot stone or upturned tray, as it will produce a better loaf this way.

BENEFITS OF USING A DUTCH OVEN

Baking your bread inside a Dutch oven (cast-iron pot) enhances the dough's oven spring, accentuates expansion through the scores on the dough, produces bigger blisters, and creates a richer color.

The Dutch oven is often used upside down; therefore, a flat-topped lid is important when looking to purchase one. The proved dough is placed in the upside-down lid and the deep base (now acting as a lid) is place over to seal. The whole thing is then placed into an oven to bake. It's like an oven within an oven. Generally, 15 minutes into the bake, the deep base is carefully removed to release the trapped steam and the loaf is left in the oven to finish baking.

If you already have a baking stone in your oven, you could use this as the base and just need to find a heavy cast-iron pot to use as the lid to encase the dough. Keep a lookout at flea markets or yard sales, as you may pick up one for peanuts. Ideally, you want a black pot as this absorbs the heat much better. Also, try to find a large rectangular heavy black pot, as this will allow for different types of breads to be baked inside. Many Dutch ovens are restrictive in what size and shape of bread can be baked within it.

HOW TO CONTROL THE FLAVOR STRENGTH OF YOUR SOURDOUGH

Sourdough breads can be strong and "tangy" or so mild you may not necessarily know they are made with a sour culture. There are many factors that influence the final flavor and aroma of sourdough bread, some of which the baker can control and steer in a predetermined direction.

Ways in which the baker can develop a strong flavor and aroma are as follows: Wild yeast and bacteria are in abundance in a healthy sour culture. Two groups of friendly bacteria, *lactic acid bacteria* (LAB) and *acetic acid bacteria* (AAB), are responsible for the type of flavor. LAB produce a rounded, creamy flavor; AAB produce sharper and tangier notes.

The lactic acid produced is also a natural preservative that inhibits the growth of harmful bacteria. Lactic fermentation increases vitamin and enzyme levels, also improving the digestibility of the fermented food. *Lactobacillus* bacteria are recognized to be beneficial for good health.

If you are aiming for a sharp and tangy flavor, then a low hydration culture kept a 68°F (20°C) will promote acetic acid production; if you require a more rounded, creamy flavor, then a high hydration culture kept at 86°F (30°C) will create more favorable conditions for lactic acid bacteria.

The length of fermentation time, from when the initial dough is formed to the time the dough enters the oven to bake, greatly affects the flavor of the final loaf. The longer the fermentation time, the stronger the flavor. Using low amounts of sour culture in your recipe, fermenting the dough in a cooler environment, and retarding the dough in the refrigerator will all extend fermentation time and increase flavor.

For some of my recipes, I recommend feeding the wheat culture twice a day for a few days before use. This produces a mildly flavored culture that is extremely active with yeast. If you bake sourdough made from this culture on the same day, it will be extremely mild in flavor. Alternatively, the same dough can be retarded in the refrigerator, which will enable the dough to start generating more pronounced flavors.

BENEFITS OF MILLING YOUR OWN GRAINS

Grains lose nutrients soon after they are milled into flour; therefore, milling grains immediately prior to making bread has nutritional benefits. The downside to this is that the breadmaking suitability of flour generally improves over time once milled, through oxidation. Because using 100 percent freshly milled flour results in heavier loaves, it is customary for only a portion of bagged flour in a recipe to be replaced with freshly milled flour.

Domestic grain mills are gaining popularity, and many home bakers have added one of these to their baking kits. The wheat is milled whenever required, so the flour will not go rancid. The coarseness of the flour can be determined by the user, as the mills can be adjusted from fine to coarse. The mills can also be used to grind ancient wheats, rice, oats, barley, and an array of dried seeds, nuts, and beans. Avoid milling oily, strongly scented, or colorful ingredients, such as coffee beans, because they will contaminate subsequent ingredients passed through the mill.

It is important to establish what type of wheat grains you can purchase locally and their suitability for breadmaking. Aim for a very strong breadmaking wheat variety and stick with the type that works for you and provides continuity in your baking.

HOW TO ADD PORRIDGE TO A DOUGH

A recent trend has been to incorporate a *porridge* into a dough to change the taste and texture of the bread. When adding a porridge to a dough, make sure the dough is lower in hydration than normal, as the moisture content and dough softness will increase when mixing in the porridge.

Crushed or flaked oats and barley are two common ingredients. My Lithuanian Keptinis con Sopracciglio (page 130) utilizes a porridge that is actually baked before being added to the fully developed dough.

When making a porridge mix, the chosen ingredient is boiled in one to two times its weight of water. Consistency should be a very thick porridge: thicker than you would normally eat for breakfast, but not too thick that it will not easily incorporate into your base dough. Once mixed, it will slowly thicken, so allow some time to judge the consistency before adding more water to the porridge.

Leftover bread can be toasted, broken up, and then soaked into a porridge. This is a smart way to prevent food waste. Toasting old sourdough bread for porridge will impart great flavors to the bread it will be baked in.

As a guide, 15 to 50 percent of porridge to flour weight is used. As the porridge quantity is increased, the more the dough consistency will soften; therefore, I recommend adding the lower percentage when making your first loaves and then gradually increase the levels as you feel comfortable handling the dough.

HOW TO MAKE HEALTHY BOTANICAL DRINKS

By making the Orange and Madagascar Vanilla botanical water as used in the panettone recipe (page 100), we have simultaneously created a wonderful, healthy drink. You can either drink it neat, although for some this is too strong, or—as is my preference—combine it with an equal amount of chilled carbonated water to make a refreshing beverage. The flavor options you can create are endless if you combine different fruits, herbs, and spices.

These fermented drinks contain probiotic bacteria. The friendly bacteria help digest our food more effectively, plus they help us absorb more nutrients from the food we eat. They also help with our immune system by keeping harmful bacteria at bay. So many positives come from such a simple thing to make.

At Cinnamon Square, when making our botanical breads and bakes, we utilize the active fermentation to leaven our products, but then we bake them to finish the process. Unfortunately, this baking kills off the yeast and bacteria and therefore no probiotic activity survives in the baked product. So, at home, you can make extra botanical water for drinking as well as baking.

CHAPTER 3
BOTANICAL
BREADS

Whether a novice or an experienced home baker, you will be blown away by the joy and sense of gratification brought by baking bread botanically. This chapter is dedicated to my favorite bread recipes, from my very first botanical bread, The Floral Loaf—originally made with magnolia petals from my garden—to the Root Vegetable Foodbank Loaf I created to utilize wonky root vegetables in wholesome, nutritious loaves of bread.

THE FLORAL LOAF

500 g (1 pound 1½ ounces) strong white bread flour

10 g (⅓ ounce) salt

200 g (7 ounces) magnolia petal botanical culture

330 g (11½ ounces) magnolia petal botanical water

Flour and ground rice mixture, for dusting

This magnolia petal loaf was the first botanical bread I ever made. I used magnolia petals from my garden as we have a few well-established trees, and every May we get a wonderful display of white and purple flowers. The lovely short-lived display quickly ends up as a slippery carpet of decaying blossoms. Because of their abundance, magnolia petals became my first venture into botanical fermentation. This baked loaf has a subtle floral aroma and a crispy golden crust with a soft, moist crumb. You will amaze your friends and family when you explain how you made this loaf.

1. Weigh the dry ingredients separately and place them in a large plastic bowl in the following order: flour first and then the salt.

2. Add the botanical culture, botanical water, and tap water, and combine until a dough starts to form and the sides of the bowl are clean.

3. Remove the dough from the bowl and knead on a dry work surface until it becomes smooth and elastic, approximately 15 minutes.

4. Use the windowpane test (see page 36) to check if the dough is fully developed.

5. Divide the dough into two 500 g (1 pound 1½ ounce) pieces and gently shape into round balls.

6. Place the dough balls into a lidded plastic container and leave to bulk ferment for 30 minutes.

7. Remove the dough balls from the container and gently reshape.

8. Place back into the container for another 30 minutes.

9. Remove the dough balls from the container and once again gently reshape.

10. Place back into the container for another 30 minutes.

11. Remove the dough balls from the container and form them into cylindrical shapes.

12. Place these shapes into two small proving baskets, predusted with a flour and ground rice mixture.

13. Place the proving baskets into a large, lidded plastic storage box and leave to fully prove. This could take from 2 to 4 hours, depending on the activity of the botanical culture and botanical water.

14. When fully proved, generously sprinkle some ground rice or semolina on a pizza peel or flat thin baking tray and then turn out the dough from the proving baskets.

15. Score the top with a lame or sharp knife (see page 40).

16. Slide the dough onto a baking stone or heavy baking tray in a preheated oven and steam the oven (see page 43).

17. Bake at 425°F (220°C, or gas mark 7) until golden brown, approximately 25 minutes.

18. Remove the baked loaves from the oven and place on a cooling rack.

Yield: 2 small loaves

MAGNOLIA PETAL FERMENT:

Place plenty of freshly picked magnolia petals in a jar, add some honey (approximately 5 percent of the weight of the petals), fill the jar with water, and close the lid. Allow 2 to 3 weeks for an active fermentation. You may need to add more honey to the magnolia petals during this period. You can also add more petals during this period as they will compact and turn brown during fermentation.

FLOUR HYDRATION LEVEL (PERCENTAGE WATER TO FLOUR):

Recipe provides 71.6 percent hydration.

Increase magnolia botanical water to 350 g (12$^{1}/_{2}$ ounces) to achieve 75 percent hydration.

Increase magnolia botanical water to 380 g (13$^{1}/_{2}$ ounces) to achieve 80 percent hydration.

CASSIOBURY FARM WATERCRESS LOAF

750 g (1 pound 10½ ounces) white bread flour

15 g (½ ounce) salt

300 g (10½ ounces) watercress botanical culture

225 g (8 ounces) watercress botanical water

225 g (8 ounces) tap water

A handful of roughly chopped watercress, as desired

Flour and ground rice mixture, for dusting

Located in Watford, England, Cassiobury Farm is a local customer at Cinnamon Square. A working farm with animals, it is best known for growing watercress for over 150 years. They grow the variety *Nasturtium officinale*, which delivers a strong flavor and aroma. When fermented, the watercress releases a wonderful peppery aroma that will carry through into your baked loaf. I recommend adding clumps of roughly chopped watercress to your dough, which will look stunning when you cut through the baked loaf. If this variety of watercress in unavailable in your region, simply use another variety.

1. Weigh the dry ingredients separately and place them into a large plastic bowl in the following order: flour first and then the salt.

2. Add the watercress botanical culture, watercress botanical water, tap water, and some watercress and combine until a dough starts to form and the sides of the bowl are clean.

3. Remove the dough from the bowl and knead on your work surface until it becomes smooth and elastic, approximately 15 minutes.

4. Use the windowpane test (see page 36) to check if the dough is fully developed.

5. Divide the dough into three 500 g (1 pound 1½ ounce) pieces and gently shape each into a round ball.

6. Place the dough balls into a lidded plastic container and leave to bulk ferment for 30 minutes.

7. Remove the dough balls from the container and gently reshape.

8. Place the dough back into the container for another 30 minutes.

9. Remove the dough balls from the container and once again gently reshape.

10. Place the dough back into the container for another 30 minutes.

11. Remove the dough balls from the container and form into cylindrical shapes.

12. Place into three small proving baskets, predusted with a flour and ground rice mixture.

13. Place the proving baskets into a large, lidded plastic storage box and leave to fully prove. This could take from 2 to 4 hours, depending on the activity of the botanical culture and botanical water.

14. When fully proved, generously sprinkle some ground rice or semolina on a pizza peel or flat thin baking tray and then turn out the dough from the proving baskets.

15. Score the top with a lame or sharp knife (see page 40).

16. Slide the dough onto a baking stone or heavy baking tray in a preheated oven and steam the oven (see page 43).

17. Bake at 425°F (220°C, or gas mark 7) until golden brown, approximately 25 minutes.

18. Remove the baked loaves from the oven and place on a cooling rack.

Yield: 3 small loaves

WATERCRESS FERMENT:

Place plenty of freshly picked watercress into your jar, add some honey (approximately 5 percent of the weight of the watercress), fill the jar with water, and close the lid. Allow 2 to 3 weeks for an active fermentation. You may need to add more honey to the watercress during this period. You may also need to add more watercress as it compacts during fermentation. This will give the fermentation a boost too.

TIP:

The added watercress will contain a lot of water, so hold back some recipe water if you do not like your dough too wet.

FLOUR HYDRATION LEVEL (PERCENTAGE WATER TO FLOUR):

Recipe provides 66 percent hydration.

Increase watercress botanical water to 350 g (12^1/$_2$ ounces) to achieve 70 percent hydration.

Increase watercress botanical water to 380 g (13^1/$_2$ ounces) to achieve 75 percent hydration.

These levels do not consider the moisture from the added watercress.

FRENCH BAGUETTES

395 g (14 ounces) French baguette flour	110 g (4 ounces) apple botanical water
10 g (1/3 ounce) salt	110 g (4 ounces) tap water
355 g (12 1/2 ounces) apple botanical culture	Rye flour, for dusting

French bakers spend years mastering the technique to make the perfect baguette. The beautiful sight of the inside dough bursting through the crispy outer cuts and an internal crumb structure containing large open pockets of air woven together with a silky mesh of dough—that is their reward. Follow my recipe, and with a little practice, you too can bring a little bit of France into your kitchen. This recipe uses apples, which are probably the simplest and most versatile ingredients to ferment.

1. Weigh the dry ingredients separately and place them into a large plastic bowl in the following order: flour first and then the salt.

2. Add the apple botanical culture, apple botanical water, and tap water and combine until a dough starts to form and the sides of the bowl are clean.

3. Remove the dough from the bowl and knead on your work surface until it becomes smooth and elastic, approximately 12 to 15 minutes.

4. Gently shape the dough into a round ball.

5. Place the dough into a lidded plastic container and leave to bulk ferment for 30 minutes.

6. Remove the dough from the container. Very gently stretch the dough and fold it into thirds.

7. Place back into the container and let it rest for another 30 minutes.

8. Remove the dough from the container and divide it into three 320 g (11 1/3 ounce) pieces. Gently form them into cylindrical shapes without squashing all the bubbles inside the dough.

9. Place smooth-side up in the container and leave for 20 minutes to allow the dough to relax before shaping the baguette.

10. Elongate the dough to the length of your choice, but remember that it needs to fit into your oven. I like to generously dust the top of the baguette with rye flour, as this gives a lovely rustic look to the baked baguette.

11. Line a baking sheet with a tea towel. Place a strip of baking paper (the length of the baguette and twice the width) on the tea towel and then place the baguette on the paper. Fold the tea towel so it cradles the baguette for support as it proves. Place the other two baguettes on the tray in the same manner next to each other.

12. Place the tray into a large, lidded plastic storage box and leave to reach three-quarter proof. This could take from 2 to 4 hours, depending on the activity of your ferment.

13. When three-quarter proved, score the top surface with a sharp knife (or lame) diagonally 4 or 5 times, approximately 1/4 inch (6 mm) deep. After the first cut, start cutting the remaining slashes halfway down from the start of the previous cut (see page 40).

TIP:

After the final feed of the botanical culture, leave it for 12 hours before using in the dough. The longer time will allow the botanical culture to impart extensibility to the dough, which is helpful when shaping into long baguettes.

TIP:

Domestic oven-size fluted baking trays are ideal for proving the dough pieces, as they provide support to the expanding dough.

TIP:

To make the cutting of your proved baguette dough easier when using a lame, I recommend refrigerating the dough pieces beforehand. This will also help you achieve the wonderful bursting (referred to as the *eyebrows*) through the cuts. The proved dough can be baked straight from your fridge.

14. Carefully lift each baguette out of the tea towel by grabbing both ends of the baking paper and pulling it taut. Place the dough and baking paper into the preheated oven onto a hot baking stone or upturned baking tray. Steam the oven (see page 43).

15. Bake at 425°F (220°C or gas mark 7) until golden brown, approximately 20 to 25 minutes.

16. Remove from the oven and place on a cooling rack.

Yield: 3 small baguettes

APPLE FERMENT:

Chop your choice of organic apples into quarters and place into your fermenting jar. I like to use Bramley apples, a traditional British cooking apple, as they are not too sweet. Cover them with water and close the lid. This should ferment very quickly and should not require the addition of honey.

FLOUR HYDRATION LEVEL (PERCENTAGE WATER TO FLOUR):

Recipe provides 697 percent hydration.

Increase the apple botanical water to 140 g (5 ounces) to achieve 75 percent hydration.

FIG AND FENNEL FARMHOUSE LOAF

500 g (1 pound 1½ ounces) white bread flour

10 g (⅓ ounce) salt

200 g (7 ounces) fig and fennel botanical culture

166 g (6 ounces) fig and fennel botanical water

100 g (3½ ounces) tap water

100 g (3½ ounces) chopped soft ready-to-eat figs

White vegetable shortening, for greasing loaf pans

Whole wheat flour, for dusting

This is one of my favorite flavored breads, which is strange, considering I do not generally eat figs or fennel. When these two ingredients are fermented together, however, they produce a delightful, sweet, mild aniseed aroma that transfers exquisitely to the bread made from it. The botanical water tastes stunning too.

I like to add chopped, soft ready-to-eat figs to the dough, to give random bursts of intense flavor and visual appeal to the cut bread slices.

1. Weigh the dry ingredients separately and place them into a large plastic bowl in the following order: flour first and then the salt.

2. Add the botanical culture, botanical water, and tap water and combine until a dough starts to form and the sides of the bowl are clean.

3. Remove the dough from the bowl and knead on a dry work surface until it becomes smooth and elastic, approximately 15 minutes.

4. Flatten the dough and sprinkle a layer of the figs on top. Roll up the dough and gently knead until the figs are evenly dispersed. Be careful not to damage the figs or their sugar will leach out into the dough, causing your bread to bake very dark.

5. Divide the dough into two 550 g (19½ ounce) pieces and gently shape into round balls.

6. Place into a lidded plastic container and leave to bulk ferment for 30 minutes.

7. Remove the dough balls from the container and gently reshape.

8. Place the dough back into the container for another 30 minutes.

9. Remove the dough balls from the container and once again gently reshape.

10. Place the dough back into the container for another 30 minutes.

11. Remove the dough balls from the container and form into cylindrical shapes.

12. Place the dough into two small farmhouse loaf pans, lightly greased with white vegetable shortening.

13. Place the loaf pans inside a large, lidded plastic storage box and leave to fully prove. This could take from 2 to 4 hours, depending on the activity of your botanical culture and botanical water.

14. When fully proved, generously sprinkle some whole wheat flour on top of the loaves.

15. Cut down the center of both dough pieces (see page 40).

16. Place both loaf pans into your preheated oven and steam the oven (see page 43).

17. Bake at 425°F (220°C, or gas mark 7) until golden brown, approximately 25 minutes.

18. Remove the baked loaves from their pans and place on a cooling rack.

Yield: 2 farmhouse loaves

FIG AND FENNEL FERMENT:

To build my ferment, I use fresh ripe figs chopped into quarters and fresh fennel chopped into thick slices. Place the figs and fennel in a fermenting jar, cover with water, and close the lid. This should not require the addition of honey as there should be enough sugar available for the yeast to enjoy.

FLOUR HYDRATION LEVEL (PERCENTAGE WATER TO FLOUR):

Recipe provides 61 percent hydration

Increase fig and fennel botanical water to 190 g (6³/₄ ounces) to achieve 65 percent hydration.

Increase fig and fennel botanical water to 220 g (7³/₄ ounces) to achieve 70 percent hydration.

Increase fig and fennel botanical water to 250 g (8³/₄ ounces) to achieve 75 percent hydration.

ROOT VEGETABLE FOODBANK LOAF

1500 g (3 pounds 5 ounces) white bread flour	450 g (1 pound) root vegetable botanical water
30 g (1 ounce) salt	450 g (1 pound) tap water
600 g (1 pound 5¼ ounces) root vegetable botanical culture	White vegetable shortening, for greasing loaf pans

I make loaves of this root vegetable botanical bread weekly and donate them to our local foodbank. Root vegetables such as potatoes, sweet potatoes, and carrots ferment easily and do not impart significant flavor to the baked loaf, making the final product more palatable for children. I bake these in small loaf pans as the resulting loaves have a soft golden crust and a wonderfully moist crumb, ideal for sandwiches and toast. This recipe will provide you with a batch of wholesome white loaves perfect for your everyday use, or you too could drop a few down at your local foodbank.

1. Weigh the dry ingredients separately and place them into a large plastic bowl in the following order: flour first and then the salt.

2. Add the botanical culture, botanical water, and tap water and combine until a dough starts to form and the sides of the bowl are clean.

3. Remove the dough from the bowl and knead on a dry work surface until it becomes smooth and elastic, approximately 15 minutes.

4. Use the windowpane test (see page 36) to check if the dough is fully developed.

5. Divide the dough into six 500 g (1 pound 1½ ounce) pieces and gently shape these into round balls.

6. Place the dough balls into a lidded plastic container and leave to bulk ferment for 30 minutes.

7. Remove the dough balls from the container and gently reshape.

8. Place the dough back into the container for another 30 minutes.

9. Remove the dough balls from the container and once again gently reshape.

10. Place the dough back into the container for another 30 minutes.

11. Remove the dough balls from the container and form them into cylindrical shapes.

12. Place each dough ball into a small loaf pan, lightly greased with white vegetable shortening.

13. Place the six loaf pans into a large, lidded plastic storage box and leave them to fully prove. This could take from 2 to 4 hours, depending on the activity of your botanical culture and botanical water.

14. When fully proved, spray water on top of the dough and, using a sharp knife, cut an incision lengthwise down the center of each of the loaves (see page 40).

15. Place the loaf pans into your preheated oven and steam the oven (see page 43).

16. Bake at 425°F (220°C, or gas mark 7) until golden brown, approximately 25 minutes.

17. Remove the baked loaves from their pans and place on a cooling rack.

Yield: 6 small split tin loaves

ROOT VEGETABLE FERMENT:
To build my ferment, I use old or less than perfect root vegetables (potato, carrot, and sweet potato) cut into thick slices. As these are grown in the ground, the vegetables must be washed to remove any dirt. Place the cut vegetables in a jar, cover them with water, and close the lid. This should not require the addition of honey as there should be enough sugars available for the yeast to enjoy.

FLOUR HYDRATION LEVEL (PERCENTAGE WATER TO FLOUR):

Recipe provides 66.6 percent hydration

Increase root vegetable botanical water to 510 g (1 pound 2 ounces) to achieve 70 percent hydration.

Increase root vegetable botanical water to 600 g (1 pound 5¼ ounces) to achieve 75 percent hydration.

VINE-RIPENED TOMATO AND BASIL PIZZA

500 g (1 pound 1 1/2 ounces) white bread flour

10 g (1/3 ounce) salt

160 g (5 3/4 ounces) vine-ripened tomato and basil botanical culture

170 g (6 ounces) vine-ripened tomato and basil botanical water

170 g (6 ounces) tap water

Semolina or ground rice, for dusting

Tomato sauce

Mozzarella cheese (or grated cheese of choice)

Pizza toppings of your choice

Extra-virgin olive oil, for brushing on dough (optional)

The key to a good pizza base is to make a long fermented, high hydration (wet) dough that is baked directly on solid stone in a very hot oven. Leave the outer edge of the pizza dough free from toppings so it will puff up in the oven to produce a delicately light and crispy pizza that would make any Italian baker proud. From this pizza base recipe, you could make a simple classic margherita pie using tomato, mozzarella, and basil, or you could create your own flavorful and colorful combination using your favorite ingredients and toppings.

1. Weigh the dry ingredients separately and place them into a large plastic bowl in the following order: flour first and then the salt.

2. Add the botanical culture, botanical water, and tap water and combine until a dough starts to form and the sides of the bowl are clean.

3. Remove the dough from the bowl and knead on a dry work surface until the dough becomes smooth and elastic, approximately 12 to 15 minutes.

4. Use the windowpane test (see page 36) to check if the dough is fully developed. This should stretch more than usual, as it will be a soft dough.

5. Gently shape the dough into a round ball.

6. Place the dough into a lidded plastic container and leave for 3 hours. Remove the dough from the container once every hour to reshape, stretch, and fold before returning to the container.

7. After the 3 hours of resting and reshaping, place the container in the fridge for approximately 12 hours to mature.

8. Remove the dough from the container and divide into four or five pieces of dough, 200 to 250 g (7 to 8 3/4 ounces) each.

9. Gently shape into round balls.

10. Place smooth-side up in a large, lidded plastic storage box for 2 to 4 hours at room temperature to double in size.

11. Gently shape each dough piece into a round on a bed of semolina or ground rice to stop it from sticking. Leave the outer edge thicker to puff up when baked.

12. Place each round of dough onto a piece of baking paper. This will help you transfer the dough to the oven.

13. Top your pizza with a layer of thick tomato sauce and grated cheese (leaving the outer edge free from any toppings) and your choice of toppings. For extra crispiness, brush the outer edge of the dough with extra-virgin olive oil before baking.

14. Slide the topped pizza dough (still on the baking paper) into the oven onto a pizza stone or an upturned heavy baking tray (both preheated in your oven) and bake at 500°F (250°C, or gas mark 10).

15. The baking time will depend on the thickness of your pizza and temperature of your oven. It may be as little as 4 to 5 minutes, so keep an eye on it.

Yield: 4 or 5 crispy pizzas

VINE-RIPENED TOMATO AND BASIL FERMENT:

To build my ferment, I use vine-ripened sweet tomatoes cut in half and freshly picked basil leaves. Place the tomatoes and basil leaves into a fermenting jar, cover them with water, and close the lid. This will usually ferment very quickly.

FLOUR HYDRATION LEVEL (PERCENTAGE WATER TO FLOUR):

Recipe provides 72.5 percent hydration.

Increase vine-ripened tomato and basil botanical water to 185 g (6¹/₂ ounces) to achieve 75 percent hydration.

POSH CUCUMBER BURGER BUNS

400 g (14 ounces) strong white bread flour

8.5 g (1/3 ounce) salt

24 g (3/4 ounce) caster sugar

60 g (2 ounces) white vegetable shortening, plus more for greasing

165 g (5 3/4 ounces) cucumber botanical culture

180 g (6 1/3 ounces) cucumber botanical water

Beaten egg, for brushing

Sesame seeds or mixed seeds (optional)

You will be fermenting cucumbers in preparation for making these burger buns. You'll also need some real top-quality steak burgers to complement these beauties. Alternatively, a homemade vegan patty will also feel at home nestled inside them. These buns will be strong enough to hold together when filled with a prime juicy burger but still tender when eaten. They have a slight sweetness and really excel once toasted. An equal quantity of butter can replace the white vegetable shortening, if you prefer. These buns can be baked on a flat tray, but if you can bake them in Yorkshire pudding trays, your burger buns will have a deeper shape when baked.

1. Weigh all the dry ingredients separately and place them into a large plastic bowl in the following order: flour first and then the salt, caster sugar, and vegetable shortening in separate piles on top.

2. Add the botanical culture, botanical water, and tap water, and combine until a dough starts to form and the sides of the bowl are clean.

3. Remove the dough from the bowl and knead on a dry work surface until it becomes smooth and elastic, approximately 12 to 15 minutes.

4. Use the windowpane test (see page 36) to check if the dough is fully developed.

5. Divide the dough into eight 105 g (3 3/4 ounce) pieces and gently shape them into round balls.

6. Place the dough balls into a lidded plastic container and leave to bulk ferment for 40 minutes.

7. Remove the dough balls from the container and gently reshape.

8. Place them back into the container for another 10 minutes.

9. Remove the dough balls again from the container and, using a rolling pin, gently roll them into circles slightly smaller than the indentation of the Yorkshire pudding tray or about 3 1/2 inches (9 cm) in diameter if using a baking paper-lined flat baking tray. Lightly grease the Yorkshire pudding tray by using a little white vegetable shortening on a paper towel.

10. Place the tray(s) into a large, lidded plastic storage box and leave to fully prove. This could take from 2 to 4 hours, depending on the activity of your ferment.

11. When fully proved, gently brush the tops with beaten egg (or use a handheld water spray containing egg).

12. Either leave plain or sprinkle some sesame seeds on top of the egg wash. Alternatively, use a multiseed blend (for example, sunflower, millet, flax, poppy, and pumpkin seeds) to give a real posh look to them.

13. Place the tray(s) into a preheated oven and bake at 400°F (200°C, or gas mark 6) until golden brown, approximately 12 to 15 minutes.

14. Remove the tray(s) from the oven and place on a cooling rack.

Yield: 8 burger buns

CUCUMBER FERMENT:

To build my ferment, I use homegrown cucumbers, but you can use store-bought instead. Use Kirby, Persian, or American cucumbers rather than the English variety. Chop the cucumber into small pieces, approximately 1 inch (2.5 cm) in size, place them into a fermenting jar, cover them with water, and close the lid. This will usually ferment easily, but you can add some honey to help it along.

TIP:

You can easily purchase Yorkshire pudding trays online. Look for trays that have four indentations, approximately 4 inches (10 cm) in diameter.

TIP:

Turn them into finger buns by rolling the dough pieces into finger shapes approximately 4 inches (10 cm) long (in step 9). This makes them ideal for holding sausages straight off the barbecue.

FLOUR HYDRATION LEVEL (PERCENTAGE WATER TO FLOUR):

Recipe provides 58.5 percent hydration.

400 g (14 ounces) strong white bread flour	162 g (5³/₄ ounces) date and walnut botanical culture	80 g (2³/₄ ounces) dates, chopped and presoaked in water, or (optionally) in Port
8 g (¹/₄ ounce) salt	112 g (4 ounces) date and walnut botanical water	
10 g (¹/₃ ounce) white vegetable shortening	100 g (3¹/₂ ounces) tap water	80 g (2³/₄ ounces) walnuts, broken into smaller pieces

DATE AND WALNUT LOAF

This date and walnut loaf provides a lovely accompaniment to cheese and wine, making it a perfect addition to your next dinner party. This recipe makes a firm dough that can be proved on a tray without the support of a loaf pan or a banneton. The baked loaf will have a light sweetness imparted from the dates and crunchy bites from the walnuts. I recommend eating this with strong blue cheese and some juicy red grapes—oh, and a glass of your favorite wine, of course.

1. Weigh all the dry ingredients separately and place them into a large plastic bowl in the following order: flour first and then the salt and vegetable shortening in separate piles on top.

2. Add the botanical culture, botanical water, and tap water, and combine until a dough starts to form and the sides of the bowl are clean.

3. Remove the dough from the bowl and knead on a dry work surface until it becomes smooth and elastic, approximately 12 to 15 minutes.

4. Use the windowpane test (see page 36) to check if the dough is fully developed.

5. Flatten the dough, sprinkle a layer of dates and walnuts over the surface, roll up the dough, and gently knead to start evenly distributing these additions within the dough. Try not to damage the dates because the sugar within the dates will leach out into the dough and cause the bread to darken as it bakes.

6. Gently shape the dough into a round ball.

7. Place into a lidded plastic container and leave to bulk ferment for 30 minutes.

8. Remove the dough from the container and gently reshape.

9. Place back into the container for another 30 minutes.

10. Remove the dough from the container and once again gently reshape.

11. Place back into the container for another 30 minutes.

12. Remove the dough from the container and once again gently reshape, knocking out any large bubbles.

13. Place back into the container for 10 minutes to allow the dough to relax before shaping.

14. Remove the dough from the container and shape it to make a tight, round ball with a smooth top. Place seam-side down onto a baking paper-lined baking tray.

15. Place the tray into a large, lidded plastic storage box and leave to fully prove. This could take from 2 to 4 hours, depending on the activity of the ferment. Rounded balls of dough generally take slightly longer to prove than cylindrical shapes.

DATE AND WALNUT FERMENT:

To build my ferment, I use good-quality ready-to-eat dates and walnut pieces. Chop the dates into small pieces and break any whole walnuts. Place them into a fermenting jar, cover them with water, and close the lid. This will usually ferment quickly due to the sugars within the dates.

TIP:

If the crust is getting too dark, lay a sheet of baking paper over the top of the loaf for the remainder of the baking time.

TIP:

Try soaking the dates in Port before adding them to the dough. This will add juicy pockets of flavor to the baked bread.

FLOUR HYDRATION LEVEL (PERCENTAGE WATER TO FLOUR):

Recipe provides 61 percent hydration.

Increase date and walnut botanical water to 130 g (4^1/$_2$ ounces) to achieve 65 percent hydration.

Increase date and walnut botanical water to 155 g (5^1/$_2$ ounces) to achieve 70 percent hydration.

Increase date and walnut botanical water to 180 g (6^1/$_3$ ounces) to achieve 75 percent hydration.

16. When fully proved, carefully cut a cross into the top surface (see page 40) and place into a preheated oven and steam the oven (see page 43).

17. Bake at 425°F (220°C, or gas mark 7) until golden brown, approximately 25 minutes. This bread may obtain a dark crust quickly due to the sugars in the dates.

18. Remove the baked loaf from your oven and place on a cooling rack.

Yield: 1 large round loaf

STILTON AND RAISIN LOAF

400 g (14 ounces) strong white bread flour	170 g (6 ounces) raisin botanical culture	90 g (3¼ ounces) raisins, soaked and drained to soften after weighing
8 g (¼ ounces) salt	115 g (4 ounces) raisin botanical water	90 g (3¼ ounces) Stilton cheese, broken up into small chunks
10 g (⅓ ounces) white vegetable shortening	100 g (3½ ounces) tap water	

I normally eat only strong cheeses, but I'm not so keen to eat chunks Stilton on their own. However, when dispersed within this baked loaf, their flavor becomes a bit more rounded. The addition of raisins imparts random juicy bursts, making this loaf one of my favorite breads to share with you.

You can swap the cheese for other strong hard cheeses if you prefer or if Stilton is not available in your area. This recipe makes a firm dough that can be proved on a tray without the support of a loaf pan or a banneton.

1. Weigh all the dry ingredients separately and place them into a large plastic bowl in the following order: flour first and then the salt and vegetable shortening in separate piles on top.

2. Add the botanical culture, botanical water, and tap water, and combine until a dough starts to form and the sides of the bowl are clean.

3. Remove the dough from the bowl and knead on a dry work surface until the dough becomes smooth and elastic, approximately 12 to 15 minutes.

4. Use the windowpane test (see page 36) to check if the dough is fully developed.

5. Flatten the dough, sprinkle a layer of raisins over the surface, roll up the dough, and gently knead to start evenly distributing the raisins within the dough, trying not to damage the raisins. When nearly completely mixed, add the chunks of Stilton cheese and start to blend them into the dough. It is good to have random-size chunks of cheese.

6. Divide the dough into two equal pieces, approximately 365 g (13 ounces) each, and gently shape each into a round ball.

7. Place into a lidded plastic container and leave to bulk ferment for 30 minutes.

8. Remove the dough from the container and gently reshape.

9. Place back into the container for another 30 minutes.

10. Remove the dough from the container and once again gently reshape.

11. Place the dough back into the container for another 30 minutes.

12. Remove the dough from the container and once again gently reshape, knocking out any large bubbles.

13. Place back into the container for 10 minutes to allow the dough to relax before shaping.

14. Form each ball of dough into a tapered cylindrical shape (thicker in the middle and thinner at the ends).

15. Place seam-side down onto a baking paper-lined baking tray.

16. Place the tray into a large, lidded plastic storage box and leave to fully prove. This could take from 2 to 4 hours, depending on the activity of the ferment.

17. When fully proved, score the tops of both loaves (see page 40). Place them into a preheated oven and steam the oven (see page 43).

RAISIN FERMENT:

To build my ferment, I use good-quality, ready-to-eat raisins. Place the raisins into a fermenting jar, cover them with water, and close the lid. This will usually ferment quickly due to the sugars within the raisins.

TIP :

Try soaking the raisins in Port before adding them to the dough. This will add juicy pockets of flavor to the baked bread.

FLOUR HYDRATION LEVEL (PERCENTAGE WATER TO FLOUR):

Recipe provides 61.8 percent hydration.

Increase raisin botanical water to 130 g (4^{1}/$_{2}$ ounces) to achieve 65 percent hydration.

Increase raisin botanical water to 155 g (5^{1}/$_{2}$ ounces) to achieve 70 percent hydration.

Increase raisin botanical water to 179 g (6^{1}/$_{3}$ ounces) to achieve 75 percent hydration.

18. Bake at 425°F (220°C, or gas mark 7) until golden brown, approximately 20 minutes. This bread will obtain a dark crust quickly due to the cheese, and burnt cheese may erupt from the dough as it expands and bakes.

19. Remove the loaves from the oven and place them on a cooling rack.

Yield: 2 small loaves

KALAMATA OLIVE CIABATTA

620 g (22 ounces) strong white bread flour

15 g (½ ounce) salt

275 g (9¾ ounces) Kalamata olive botanical culture

195 g (7 ounces) Kalamata olive botanical water

195 g (7 ounces) tap water

Extra-virgin olive oil, for greasing

Ground rice, for dusting

Ciabatta is made from a very soft, sticky dough that requires a different method of kneading. The soft dough is instrumental in producing the characteristic large-holed internal structure and crispy crust for this classical Italian bread. This recipe starts with a flour hydration of 70 percent to help you get used to kneading a soft dough. Normally, ciabatta would be made with at least 75 percent hydration.

The addition of Kalamata olives (see Tip on page 71) to the dough complements the botanical ferment and looks attractive throughout the baked ciabatta.

1. Weigh the dry ingredients separately and place them into a large plastic bowl in the following order: flour first and then the salt.

2. Add the botanical culture, botanical water, and tap water. Then, using one hand, bring the ingredients together until a very wet, sticky dough is just formed.

3. Turn out the wet mixture onto the table and knead, using the slap-and-fold method (see page 34), until it is smooth and elastic. Continue kneading for at least 10 minutes.

4. Use the windowpane test (see page 36) to check if the dough is fully developed. This should stretch way more than a regular lower hydration dough stretches.

5. At the point when the dough feels smooth and extensible, form it into a cylindrical shape.

6. Place into a lidded, plastic rectangular container, approximately 12 x 7 inches (30.5 x 18 cm), whose bottom and sides have been lightly greased with extra-virgin olive oil, and leave to bulk ferment for 30 minutes.

7. Remove the dough from the plastic container. Gently stretch and fold it into thirds. Then gently flatten it to fit the base of the container. You can use a rolling pin to give a neater shape as you flatten it.

8. Place the dough back into the container and leave it for another 30 minutes.

9. Sprinkle a generous layer of the Flour and Rice Dressing (see note) on your work surface large enough for the dough to sit on.

10. Carefully turn out the dough from the container onto the bed of Flour and Rice Dressing.

11. Sprinkle a generous layer of the Flour and Rice Dressing over the top of the dough.

12. Using a metal scraper, cut the dough into rectangles approximately 2 x 6 inches (5 x 15 cm). Quickly and firmly pressing the metal scraper through the dough to the work surface, rather than using a sawing action, to cause minimal damage and degassing of the dough.

13. Gently pick up and place each dough rectangle onto a baking paper-lined baking tray generously sprinkled with ground rice (to prevent the dough from sticking). Leave room for the dough to expand without touching.

FLOUR AND RICE DRESSING

This mixture is used a lot in Italian baking as a dressing for bread and as a nonstick material for wet doughs. It is also used to dust proving baskets before placing the high hydration soft dough inside to prove. Make more than you need and keep it in a jar ready to use.

200 g (7 ounces) strong white bread flour

200 g (7 ounces) ground rice

Stir together with a spoon until thoroughly blended.

KALAMATA OLIVE FERMENT:

To build my ferment, I use good-quality, dark purple Kalamata olives. Place the Kalamata olives into a fermenting jar, cover them with water, and close the lid. This will usually ferment without needing any honey.

TIP :

You can add olives to the dough for extra flavor and visual appeal. Add 260 g (9 ounces) of olives chopped in half or quarters. Drain them thoroughly and only add them once the dough is thoroughly kneaded. Fold them into the dough until they are evenly dispersed.

FLOUR HYDRATION LEVEL (PERCENTAGE WATER TO FLOUR):

Recipe provides 70 percent hydration.

Increase Kalamata olive botanical water to 230 g (8 ounces) to achieve 75 percent hydration.

Increase Kalamata olive botanical water to 268 g (9 1/2 ounces) to achieve 80 percent hydration.

Increase Kalamata olive botanical water to 305 g (10 3/4 ounces) to achieve 85 percent hydration.

14. Place the tray into a large, lidded plastic storage box and leave to fully prove. This could take from 2 to 4 hours, depending on the activity of the ferment.

15. When fully proved, place the dough into a preheated oven onto a hot baking stone or upturned baking tray and steam the oven (see page 43).

16. Bake at 425°F (220°C, or gas mark 7) until golden brown, approximately 15 minutes.

17. Remove from the oven and place on a cooling rack.

Yield: 6 to 8 ciabatta rolls

ROSEMARY, SULTANA, AND ROCK SALT FOCACCIA

335 g (11³/₄ ounces) strong white bread flour , plus more for dusting	135 g (4³/₄ ounces) rosemary and sultana botanical culture	90 g (3¹/₄ ounces) tap water
8 g (¹/₄ ounce) salt	90 g (3¹/₄ ounces) rosemary and sultana botanical water	Chopped fresh rosemary, for topping
28 g (1 ounce) extra-virgin olive oil , plus more for brushing		Flaky sea salt, for topping

This authentic Italian focaccia recipe makes the most wonderfully soft, cake-like textured bread. The dough will be very soft, like ciabatta, but not as sticky due to the high quantity of oil used. Preparing the dough for baking is unlike any other bread dough because you liberally apply a layer of water followed by copious amounts of extra-virgin olive oil. Then, you randomly press your fingers through the proved dough before generously scattering rosemary and flaky sea salt on top. You may be thinking that it sounds messy. *It is!* But in a fun way.

In Italy, focaccia is often made in large trays and are then cut and sold by weight. With this recipe, you could make either one whole baking tray or two focaccia rounds.

1. Weigh the dry ingredients separately and place them into a large plastic bowl in the following order: flour first and then the salt.

2. Add the extra-virgin olive oil, botanical culture, botanical water, and tap water. Then, using one hand, bring together until an extremely wet, sticky dough is just formed.

3. Turn out the wet mixture onto the table and knead, using the slap-and-fold method (see page 34), until it is smooth and elastic. Continue kneading for at least 10 minutes.

4. Use the windowpane test (see page 36) to check if the dough is fully developed. This should stretch way more than a regular lower hydration dough stretches.

5. When the dough feels smooth and extensible, divide it into two pieces of equal weight, approximately 325 g (11¹/₂ ounces) each, and gently shape them into round balls.

6. Place the dough balls into a lidded plastic rectangular container and leave to bulk ferment for 30 minutes.

7. Remove from the container and gently stretch and fold the dough back into round balls.

8. Place the dough balls back into the container for another 30 minutes.

9. Remove from the container and, using a rolling pin and a little flour for dusting, roll out each piece to approximately 10 inches (25.5 cm) round and place on a baking paper-lined baking tray.

10. Place the tray into a large, lidded storage box and leave to fully prove. This could take from 2 to 4 hours, depending on the activity of your ferment.

11. Remove the tray from the storage box and generously brush the top of each dough round with water and then apply another generous layer of extra-virgin olive oil.

12. Randomly press a finger vertically through the top of the dough through to the tray, approximately 10 times across the dough.

13. Place the tray back into the storage box for another 30 minutes.

ROSEMARY AND SULTANA FERMENT:

To build my ferment, I use good-quality ready-to-eat sultanas, or golden raisins, and freshly picked rosemary. Place the sultanas and rosemary into a fermenting jar, cover them with water, and close the lid. This will usually ferment quickly due to the sugars within the sultanas.

TIP:

Try other topping combinations like vine-ripened cherry tomato and oregano, roasted red and yellow peppers, or black and green olives.

14. Remove the tray from the storage box and sprinkle the top of the dough with rosemary and flaky sea salt.

15. Bake at 425°F (220°C, or gas mark 7) until golden brown, approximately 15 minutes.

16. Remove from the oven, immediately brush the top of each focaccia with more extra-virgin olive oil, and leave them on the tray to cool. The oil imparts a richer color to the baked focaccia and makes them even softer to eat.

Yield: 2 focaccia rounds

FLOUR HYDRATION LEVEL (PERCENTAGE WATER TO FLOUR):

Recipe provides 61.5 percent hydration.

125 g (4⅓ ounces)
beets

500 g (1 pound
1½ ounces) white
bread flour

10 g (⅓ ounce) salt

200 g (7 ounces)
beet and lemon
botanical culture

130 g (4½ ounces)
beet and lemon
botanical water

100 g (3½ ounces)
tap water

30 g (1 ounce)
lemon juice

White vegetable
shortening, for
greasing loaf pans

BEET AND LEMON LOAF

The addition of beets produces the most vibrant colorful dough, but retaining this color is another matter. Betanin is the pigment responsible for producing the red-violet color in beets. It is difficult to retain this original color because it disappears or turns yellow when baked. To counteract this, create a very acidic dough (sourdough) or add lemon juice or vinegar to the dough and then bake the bread for the shortest time possible. The loaf you bake from this recipe will be beautifully moist and flavorful and contain little red bursts of beet, plus some extra zing from the added lemon juice. And each time you make it, you will have that moment of anticipation when you cut the first slice: what color will it be inside?

1. Wash and peel the beets and then chop them into small pieces.

2. Using a blender, blitz the beets into a pulp, leaving some small pieces intact. Set aside for use in step 7.

3. Weigh the dry ingredients separately and place them into a large plastic bowl in the following order: flour first and then the salt.

4. Add the botanical culture, botanical water, tap water, and lemon juice and combine until a dough starts to form and the sides of the bowl are clean.

5. Remove the dough from the bowl and knead on a dry work surface until it becomes smooth and elastic, approximately 15 minutes. The dough will be slightly firm until the beet pulp is added.

6. Use the windowpane test (see page 36) to check if the dough is fully developed.

7. Flatten the dough, spread the beet pulp on top, and roll up the dough.

8. Gently knead the dough until the beet pulp is fully dispersed and the dough has reformed. The dough will now feel very soft.

9. Divide the dough into two 500 g (1 pound 1½ ounce) pieces and gently shape into round balls.

10. Place into a lidded plastic container and leave to bulk ferment for 30 minutes.

11. Remove the dough balls from the container and gently reshape.

12. Place back into the container for another 30 minutes.

13. Remove the dough balls from the container and once again gently reshape.

14. Place back into the container for another 30 minutes.

15. Remove the dough balls from the container and form into cylindrical shapes.

16. Place into small baking pans, lightly greased with white vegetable shortening.

17. Place the baking pans into a large, lidded plastic storage box and leave to fully prove. This could take from 2 to 4 hours, depending on the activity of the ferment.

BEET AND LEMON FERMENT:

To build my ferment, I use organic beets and unwaxed lemons. The beets must be washed to remove any dirt. Cut the beets into quarters and the lemons in half. Place them in your fermenting jar, cover them with water, and close the lid. This should not require the addition of honey as there should be enough sugars available for the yeast to enjoy.

FLOUR HYDRATION LEVEL (PERCENTAGE WATER TO FLOUR):

Recipe provides 60 percent hydration.

Increase botanical water to 160 g (5³/₄ ounces) to achieve 65 percent hydration.

Increase botanical water to 190 g (6³/₄ ounces) to achieve 70 percent hydration.

Increase botanical water to 220 g (7³/₄ ounces) to achieve 75 percent hydration.

These levels do not take into account the moisture from the added beet.

18. When fully proved, spray water on the top of each and, using a sharp knife, cut an incision lengthwise down the center of the dough (see page 40).

19. Place the baking pans into a preheated oven and steam the oven (see page 43).

20. Bake at 425°F (220°C, or gas mark 7) until golden brown, approximately 25 minutes.

21. Remove the baked loaves from their pans and place on a cooling rack.

Yield: 2 small loaves

CHAPTER 4
BOTANICAL
SWEET BUNS

If bread is the staff of life, then buns are life's little gems. The most wonderfully tender and flavorful bakes can be made from an enriched fermented dough. The addition of jams, curds, plump fruits, nuts, and spices take this dough to another level. I have chosen many of my favorite recipes, including my signature Cinnamon Square Bun and its award-winning sibling, the Ricky Sticky Bun.

When making botanical buns, the core ingredients are the same as for botanical bread: flour, salt, botanical water, and botanical culture. A similar methodology is followed; therefore, a fully developed dough is required. The difference comes from the extra ingredients necessary to impart sweetness and softness to the buns: butter, sugar, milk, and eggs are generally the main additions.

Sugar is food for the yeast, but adding lots of sugar will inhibit yeast activity. Therefore, in a standard bun dough containing fresh or dried yeast, extra yeast is added to "speed up" the fermentation process. When making the same dough botanically, we cannot add any more yeast via the botanical water, as the dough would be too wet. For this reason, I use the botanical water at 100 percent of the total water required for the dough. This ensures maximum activity is present in the dough from the start. Warming the botanical water to 77°F to 86°F (25°C to 30°C) when making the dough will also help, as it encourages an active yeast population inside the dough.

Proving the botanical buns will take much longer compared to botanical bread. They can take up to 24 hours. I recommend you prove the dough pieces in lidded plastic containers to prevent drying out (skinning) of the dough during this extended fermentation time. Be patient, and the reward will be sweet and fruitful.

SICILIAN LEMON AND RAISIN BELGIAN BUNS

Here, a spiral of sweet and tender botanical dough is rolled together with a generous smear of tangy lemon curd and plump, juicy raisins. Delicately baked to retain the softness, the bun is then topped with a silky-smooth white icing and finished with the iconic glacé cherry in the middle.

1. Weigh all the dry ingredients separately and place them into a large plastic bowl in the following order: flour first and then the salt, caster sugar, and milk powder in separate piles on top.

2. Thoroughly stir the ingredients together to fully disperse the milk powder and prevent any lumps from forming once the liquid is added.

3. Add the butter, botanical culture, and botanical water and combine until a dough starts to form and the sides of the bowl are clean.

4. Remove the dough from the bowl and knead on a dry work surface until the dough becomes smooth and elastic, approximately 15 minutes.

5. Use the windowpane test (see page 36) to check if the dough is fully developed.

6. Gently shape the dough into a rectangle.

7. Place into a lidded plastic container and leave to bulk ferment for 30 minutes.

8. Remove the dough from the container, lightly stretch it, and fold it into thirds.

9. Place the dough back into the container for another 30 minutes.

10. Remove the dough from the container and repeat the stretch and fold.

11. Place the dough back into the container for another 30 minutes.

12. Remove the dough from the container and, using a rolling pin, roll it into a 15 x 10-inch (40 x 25.5 cm) rectangle. Rotate the dough so it is positioned with the 15-inch (40 cm) edge closest to you.

13. Spread the lemon curd over the top of the dough, leaving the edge closest to you bare. You can use more or less of the lemon curd if you prefer.

14. Sprinkle the raisins evenly onto the lemon curd and lightly press in to keep them in place as you roll up the dough.

15. Lightly wet the edge that does not have the curd on it.

16. From the edge furthest away from you, start to roll up the dough into a 15-inch (40 cm)-long cylindrical shape of uniform thickness.

17. Mark the top every $1^1/2$ inches (4 cm) with a knife.

18. Using a long, sharp serrated knife, gently cut the dough along these marks into 10 pieces. Use a sawing motion to prevent squashing the rolled dough.

Continues...

500 g (1 pound 1½ ounces) strong white bread flour	200 g (7 ounces) Sicilian lemon and raisin botanical culture	160 g (5¾ ounces) raisins (presoaked in water and drained)
5 g (⅙ ounce) salt	235 g (8¼ ounces) Sicilian lemon and raisin botanical water	Beaten egg, for brushing over the top
50 g (1¾ ounces) caster sugar		Poured fondant icing, for decoration
20 g (⅔ ounce) milk powder	130 g (4½ ounces) lemon curd	
80 g (2¾ ounces) softened unsalted butter		Glacé cherries, for decoration

SICILIAN LEMON AND RAISIN FERMENT:

To build my ferment, I use unwaxed organic lemons (Sicilian, if available) and good-quality, ready-to-eat raisins. Cut the lemons into quarters, place them and the raisins into a fermenting jar, cover the ingredients with water, and close the lid. This will usually ferment quickly due to the sugars within the raisins.

19. Place each portion (spiral facing upward) on a baking paper–lined baking tray. Make sure to leave enough space around each one for expansion while proving and baking, so that when fully baked, the buns are not fused together. This may require two trays.

20. Place the tray into a large, lidded plastic storage box and leave to fully prove. This could take from 3 to 6 hours, depending upon the activity of the ferment.

21. When fully proved, remove the tray from the storage box, gently brush the tops of the buns with beaten eggs, and bake at 425°F (220°C, or gas mark 7) for approximately 10 to 12 minutes.

22. Remove the tray from the oven and place on a cooling rack. The buns should be golden brown and will soften as they cool.

23. When the buns are cool, spread the poured fontant icing on top of each bun. Finish by placing the customary glacé cherry in the center.

Yield: 10 buns

TIP:

Add the zest of one lemon to the dough for extra zing.

TIP:

If you have the large Yorkshire pudding trays (with four indentations per tray), you can prove and bake the Belgian buns in these rather than on a flat tray. This ensures each bun will be the same diameter, plus the buns will be taller than those baked directly on a flat tray.

TIP:

The fermenting liquid also makes a lovely refreshing drink; combine equal parts lemon and raisin botanical water and chilled sparkling water and enjoy.

FLOUR HYDRATION LEVEL (PERCENTAGE WATER TO FLOUR):

Recipe provides 55.8 percent hydration.

AWARD-WINNING CINNAMON SQUARE BUNS

The Cinnamon Square Bun is the signature product of my bakery. It's a sweet fermented dough rolled up with a buttery sweet cinnamon filling and topped with a divine cream cheese frosting. This bun is so good that it has won four national awards to date.

Although cinnamon buns are lovely to eat at room temperature, I always recommend eating them warm, either soon after exiting the oven or reheated in the microwave to keep them soft and gooey.

In this botanical version, I ferment raisins with cinnamon sticks. If you enjoy eating raisins, then you could sprinkle some whole ones over the filling before you roll up the dough (step 12).

You will need a 9-inch (23 cm) square baking pan.

1. Weigh all the dry ingredients separately and place them into a large plastic bowl in the following order: flour first and then the caster sugar, salt, and milk powder in separate piles on top.

2. Thoroughly stir the ingredients together to fully disperse the milk powder to prevent any lumps from forming once the liquid is added.

3. Add the botanical culture, botanical water, and tap water, and combine until a dough starts to form and the sides of the bowl are clean.

4. Remove the dough from the bowl and knead on a dry work surface until the dough becomes smooth and elastic, approximately 12 to 15 minutes. Expect the dough to feel firm as you knead. When the butter is added in step 6, it will soften.

5. Use the windowpane test (see page 36) to check if the dough is fully developed.

6. Place the dough back in the plastic bowl and add the butter. Using one hand, start squeezing the butter into the dough. It may take a little while, but keep persevering.

7. After the butter is fully incorporated, place the dough on the work surface and knead until it feels smooth and elastic.

8. Form the dough into a cylindrical shape.

9. Place into a lidded plastic container and leave to bulk ferment for 30 minutes.

10. Remove the dough from the container and gently shape it into a rectangle.

11. Place the dough back in the container for another 30 minutes.

12. Remove the dough from the container and, using a rolling pin, roll the dough into an 8 x 14-inch (20 x 35.5 cm) rectangle. Rotate the dough so it is positioned with the 8-inch (20 cm) edge closest to you.

13. Using a pallet knife, also called an offset spatula, spread the Cinnamon Bun Filling over the dough, leaving the edge closest to you free from any filling.

14. Press flat the edge closest to you and lightly spray with water.

15. Starting from the end furthest from you, roll up the dough into an 8-inch (20 cm)-long cylindrical shape of uniform thickness.

Continues…

DOUGH:

250 g (8³/₄ ounces) strong white bread flour

25 g (1 ounce) caster sugar

Pinch salt

10 g (¹/₃ ounce) milk powder

100 g (3¹/₂ ounces) cinnamon and raisin botanical culture

120 g (4¹/₄ ounces) cinnamon and raisin botanical water

25 g (1 ounce) softened unsalted butter

CINNAMON BUN FILLING:

100 g (3¹/₂ ounces) caster sugar

50 g (1³/₄ ounces) softened unsalted butter

10 g (¹/₃ ounce) ground cinnamon

Combine the ingredients in a medium bowl with a spoon until thoroughly mixed together.

FLOUR HYDRATION LEVEL (PERCENTAGE WATER TO FLOUR):

Recipe provides 567 percent hydration.

CREAM CHEESE FROSTING:

50 g (1³/4 ounces) cream cheese

125 g (4¹/3 ounces) icing sugar

15 g (¹/2 ounce) softened unsalted butter

Combine the ingredients in a medium bowl with a spoon until thoroughly mixed together. Do not overmix, as the frosting will soften too much.

CINNAMON AND RAISIN FERMENT:

To build my ferment, I use a few cinnamon sticks and good-quality, ready-to-eat raisins. Place the cinnamon sticks and the raisins into a fermenting jar, cover them with water, and close the lid. This will usually ferment quickly due to the sugars within the raisins.

TIP:

You can freeze the whole tray with the topping on. Make sure they are cut before freezing and then you can take one out at a time to enjoy.

16. Using a long, sharp serrated knife, cut four 2-inch (5 cm) buns. Use a sawing motion to prevent squashing the rolled dough pieces.

17. Place the buns, swirl-side up, into a baking paper–lined 9-inch (23 cm) square baking pan.

18. Place the baking pan into a large, lidded plastic storage box to fully prove. This could take from 3 to 6 hours, depending on the activity of the ferment.

19. When fully proved, remove from the storage box and bake in a preheated oven at 400°F (200°C, or gas mark 6) for 8 to 12 minutes.

20. Remove the tray from the oven and place on a cooling rack.

21. Approximately 15 to 20 minutes after removing the buns from the oven, spread the Cream Cheese Frosting over the buns.

22. The frosting should soften a little and run into the buns, but at the same time, leave a nice layer on top.

23. They are now ready to eat—warm and gooey!

Yield: 4 buns

ORANGE, LEMON, AND CURRANTS CHELSEA BUNS

FLOUR
HYDRATION LEVEL
(PERCENTAGE
WATER TO FLOUR):

Recipe provides
56.5 percent hydration.

Continues...

DOUGH:

250 g (8³/4 ounces) strong white bread flour

25 g (1 ounce) caster sugar

3 g (pinch) salt

10 g (¹/3 ounce) milk powder

10 g (¹/3 ounce) egg yolk (at room temperature)

120 g (4¹/4 ounces) botanical orange, lemon, and currant culture

110 g (4 ounces) botanical orange, lemon, and currant water

35 g (1¹/4 ounces) softened unsalted butter

Beaten egg, for bushing over the top

Demerara sugar, for decoration

CHELSEA BUN FILLING:

100 g (3¹/2 ounces) demerara sugar

50 g (1³/4 ounces) softened unsalted butter

Combine both ingredients in a small bowl with a spoon until thoroughly mixed together.

A long time classic bun, these are commonplace in most traditional bakeries in England. This sweet fermented bun is rolled into a spiral containing a swirling ribbon of rich, buttery paste with juicy currants and candied citrus peels. The filling also imparts a chewy toffee-like base to the bun as it caramelizes while baking.

You will need a 9-inch (23 cm) square baking pan.

1. Weigh all the dry ingredients separately and place them into a large plastic bowl in the following order: flour first and then the caster sugar, salt, and milk powder in separate piles on top.

2. Thoroughly stir the ingredients together to fully disperse the milk powder to prevent any lumps from forming once the liquid is added.

3. Add the egg yolk, botanical culture, and botanical water, and combine until a dough starts to form and the sides of the bowl are clean.

4. Remove the dough from the bowl and knead on your work surface until it becomes smooth and elastic, approximately 12 to 15 minutes. Expect the dough to feel firm as you knead. When the butter is added in step 6, the dough will soften.

5. Use the windowpane test (see page 36) to check if the dough is fully developed.

6. Place the dough back in the plastic bowl and add the butter. Using one hand, start squeezing the butter into the dough. It may take a little while but keep persevering.

7. After the butter is fully incorporated, place the dough on your work surface and knead until it feels smooth and elastic.

8. Form the dough into a cylindrical shape.

9. Place into a lidded plastic container and leave to bulk ferment for 50 minutes.

10. Remove the dough from the container and, using a rolling pin, roll the dough into an 8 x 14-inch (20 x 35.5 cm) rectangle.

11. Rotate the dough so it is positioned with the 8-inch (20 cm) edge closest to you.

12. Using a pallet knife, spread the Chelsea Bun Filling over the dough, leaving the edge closest to you free from any filling.

13. Sprinkle the Chelsea Bun Dried Fruits Mixture over the top and lightly press into the Chelsea Bun Filling.

14. Press the edge closest to you flat and lightly spray with water.

15. Starting from the end furthest from you, roll the dough into an 8-inch (20 cm)-long cylindrical shape of uniform thickness.

CHELSEA BUN DRIED FRUITS MIXTURE:

100 g (3½ ounces) currants, presoaked and drained

15 g (½ ounce) freshly grated orange and lemon peel

Combine the currants and mixed peel in a small bowl until thoroughly mixed together.

ORANGE, LEMON, AND CURRANTS FERMENT:

To build my ferment, I chop the oranges and lemons into quarters and add good-quality, dried currants. Place the oranges, lemons, and currants into a fermenting jar, cover them with water, and close the lid. This will usually ferment quickly due to the sugars within all the ingredients.

16. Using a long, sharp serrated knife, cut four 2-inch (5 cm) buns. Use a sawing motion to prevent squashing the rolled dough pieces.

17. Place the buns, swirl-side up, into a baking paper–lined 9-inch (23 cm) square baking pan.

18. Place the baking pan into a large, lidded plastic storage box to fully prove. This could take from 3 to 6 hours, depending on the activity of the ferment.

19. When fully proved, remove the baking pan from the storage box, brush the top of each bun with beaten egg, place the pan into the preheated oven, and bake at 400°F (200°C, or gas mark 6) for 8 to 12 minutes. Look down between the buns to make sure they are not raw at the bottom.

20. Remove the buns from your oven and immediately sprinkle with the demerara sugar.

21. Place on a cooling rack.

Yield: 4 buns

STRAWBERRY AND MADAGASCAR VANILLA SWISS FINGER BUNS

Another classic sweet fermented bun, these finger-shaped buns are simply topped with a poured fondant icing. These are simple but totally irresistible once you have made them. The beauty with these buns is that you can get really carried away by adding fillings—such as freshly whipped cream, jams, curds, or ganache—and then toppings—including chocolate fudge, nuts, sprinkles—or even trying a feathering decoration with your icing. They just get even more irresistible!

1. Weigh all the dry ingredients separately and place them into a large plastic bowl in the following order: flour first and then the caster sugar, salt, and milk powder in separate piles on top.

2. Thoroughly stir the ingredients together to fully disperse the milk powder and prevent any lumps from forming once the liquid is added.

3. Add the egg yolk, botanical culture, and botanical water and combine until a dough starts to form and the sides of the bowl are clean.

4. Remove the dough from the bowl and knead on a dry work surface until it becomes smooth and elastic, approximately 12 to 15 minutes. Expect the dough to feel firm as you knead. When the butter is added in step 6, the dough will soften.

5. Use the windowpane test (see page 36) to check if the dough is fully developed.

6. Place the dough back in your plastic bowl and add the butter. Using one hand, start squeezing the butter into the dough. It may take a little while but keep persevering.

7. After the butter is fully incorporated, place the dough on the work surface and knead until it feels smooth and elastic.

8. Divide the dough into ten 75 g (2³⁄₄ ounce) pieces and gently shape them into round balls.

9. Place the dough balls into a lidded plastic container and leave to bulk ferment for 30 minutes.

10. Remove the dough balls from the container and gently reshape.

11. Place back into the container for another 30 minutes.

12. Remove the dough balls from the container and once again gently reshape.

13. Place back into the container and leave for another 10 minutes.

14. Remove the dough balls from the container and elongate by rolling each piece under your hand into a cylindrical shape approximately 4 inches (10 cm) long.

15. Place the cylinders on a baking paper-lined baking tray. Make sure to leave enough space around each one for expansion while proving and baking, so that when fully baked, the buns are not fused together. This may require two trays.

Continues...

355 g (12¹/₂ ounces) strong white bread flour

35 g (1¹/₄ ounces) caster sugar

4 g (2 pinches) salt

10 g (¹/₃ ounce) milk powder

10 g (¹/₃ ounce) egg yolk (at room temperature)

160 g (5³/₄ ounces) botanical strawberry and Madagascar vanilla culture

160 g (5³/₄ ounces) botanical strawberry and Madagascar vanilla water

50 g (1³/₄ ounces) softened unsalted butter

Poured fondant icing, for decoration

Fillings, such as jams, curds, ganache, or whipped fresh cream (optional)

FLOUR HYDRATION LEVEL (PERCENTAGE WATER TO FLOUR):

Recipe provides 56.3 percent hydration.

To build my ferment, I chop fresh organic strawberries in half and add a couple of Madagascar vanilla pods cut into thirds. Place the strawberries and Madagascar vanilla pods into a fermenting jar, cover them with water, and close the lid. This will usually ferment quickly due to the sugars in the strawberries.

16. Place the tray into a large, lidded plastic storage box and leave to fully prove. This could take from 3 to 6 hours, depending on the activity of the ferment.

17. When fully proved, remove the tray from the storage box and bake at 400°F (200°C, or gas mark 6) for 8 to 12 minutes. The buns will be golden brown and will soften as they cool down.

18. Remove the tray from your oven and place on a cooling rack.

19. When cool, dip the top of each bun in the poured fondant icing (which can be colored and flavored if preferred).

20. When the icing is set, you can get creative by gently cutting each bun horizontally in half and then adding your chosen filling(s).

Yield: 10 buns

CURRANTS, SULTANAS, CINNAMON, CLOVE, AND NUTMEG HOT CROSS BUNS

FLOUR HYDRATION LEVEL (PERCENTAGE WATER TO FLOUR):

Recipe provides 58.6 percent hydration.

Continues...

DOUGH:

280 g (10 ounces) strong white bread flour	5 g (1/6 ounce) ground cinnamon	140 g (5 ounces) currants, sultanas, cinnamon, clove, and nutmeg botanical culture	55 g (2 ounces) softened unsalted butter	Beaten egg, for brushing over the top
3.5 g (2 pinches) salt	5 g (1/6 ounce) ground mixed spice	130 g (4 1/2 ounces) currants, sultanas, cinnamon, clove, and nutmeg botanical water	53 g (2 ounces) currants (washed and drained)	
35 g (1 1/4 ounces) caster sugar	2.5 g (pinch) ground nutmeg		53 g (2 ounces) sultanas (washed and drained)	
	10 g (1/3 ounce) egg yolk (at room temperature)			

This lightly spiced and fruited sweet bun topped with a cross is a must-bake bun for the Easter holiday. The cross is said to let the devil out and expel bad spirits, so don't forget to add it before they're baked! You will be using freshly ground spices becasue these impart a more authentic and rounded flavor. Use the plumpest fruits, as these will add a wonderful softness to every bite. I recommend cutting the baked buns in half and toasting them before applying generous amounts of creamy butter on each half.

1. Weigh all the dry ingredients separately and place them into a large plastic bowl in the following order: flour first and then the salt, caster sugar, cinnamon, mixed spice, and nutmeg in separate piles on top.

2. Add the egg yolk, the botanical culture, and the botanical water and combine until a dough starts to form and the sides of the bowl are clean.

3. Remove the dough from the bowl and knead on a dry work surface until it becomes smooth and elastic, approximately 12 to 15 minutes.

4. Use the windowpane test (see page 36) to check if the dough is fully developed.

5. Place the dough back in your plastic bowl and add the butter. Using one hand, start squeezing the butter into the dough. It may take a little while but keep persevering.

6. After the butter is fully incorporated, place the dough on the work surface and knead until it feels smooth and elastic.

7. Flatten the dough, sprinkle a layer of currants and sultanas over the surface, roll up the dough, and gently knead to start evenly distributing the fruits within the dough, trying not to damage the fruit too much as the sugar within them will leach out into the dough and cause the buns to bake very dark.

8. Divide the dough into nine 85 g (3 ounce) pieces and gently shape them into round balls.

9. Place the dough balls into a lidded plastic container and leave to bulk ferment for 30 minutes.

10. Remove the dough balls from the container and gently reshape.

11. Place back into the container for another 30 minutes.

12. Remove the dough balls from the container and once again gently reshape.

13. Place back into the container for another 10 minutes.

14. Remove the dough balls from the container, once again gently reshape, and then place them on a baking paper–lined baking tray. You can leave space around each one to expand while proving and baking in the oven without touching, or you can place them a little closer so they actually do touch, which will give a softer bake to the sides due to sticking together. If possible, place them three by three, as this will make piping the Crossing Mixture on top easier.

CURRANTS, SULTANAS, CINNAMON, CLOVE, AND NUTMEG FERMENT:

To build my ferment, I use good-quality plump currants and sultanas, cinnamon sticks, whole cloves, and whole nutmeg. Place the currants, sultanas, cinnamon sticks, whole cloves, and whole nutmeg into a fermenting jar, cover them with water, and close the lid. This will usually ferment quickly due to the sugars within the currants and sultanas. Don't add too much spice to start with. Test the flavor after a few days and if not intense enough, add some more of one or all the spices.

15. Place the tray into a large, lidded plastic storage box and leave to fully prove. This could take from 3 to 6 hours, depending on the activity of the ferment.

16. While proving, make the Crossing Mixture.

17. When fully proved, remove the tray from the storage box and gently brush the top of each dough ball with beaten egg.

18. Pipe the Crossing Mixture over the buns. Try piping in straight lines. For example, if the buns are laid out three by three in the tray, pipe three horizontal lines and then pipe three vertical lines (only stopping when you get to the end of each line). The lines should be thin as they will flow a little once piped.

19. Place the tray into a preheated oven and bake at 425°F (220°C, or gas mark 7) for 12 to 15 minutes until golden brown.

20. Remove the tray from the oven and place on a cooling rack.

Yield: 9 buns

TIP:

Add the grated zest of one orange and one lemon to give the buns a citrus note.

TIP:

Cut a small hole, 1/4 inch (6 mm) maximum, in the bottom corner of a strong sandwich bag to use as an alternative to a piping bag. Start with a very small hole and practice piping straight lines on the work surface (you can scrape this back into the bag and re-pipe). You can always increase the size of the hole if it is too small.

CROSSING MIXTURE:

150 g (5¼ ounces) strong white bread flour

30 g (1 ounce) white vegetable shortening

150 g (5¼ ounces) tap water (tepid)

1. Weigh all the dry ingredients separately and place them into a medium plastic bowl in the following order: flour first and then the white vegetable shortening on top.

2. Using your fingers, rub the vegetable shortening into the flour until no lumps can be seen.

3. Add the tap water and mix with a wooden spoon until a smooth batter is formed.

4. Place into a plastic piping bag and cut a 1/4-inch (6 mm) hole in the bottom corner.

CURRANTS, SULTANAS, AND EARL GREY TEA CAKES

A pot of tea and a toasted tea cake makes for a lovely start to the day. These cakes are made from a rich, buttery dough and packed with dried fruits. When baked, the tea cakes are best served cut in half, toasted, and smothered in butter and a dollop of your favorite jam. In this recipe, I use Earl Grey loose leaf tea in the botanical fermentation, but you could replace this with any other loose-leaf tea to personalize your own version. There are some lovely fruited and floral loose-leaf tea blends available to impart wonderful flavors and aromas to the ferment.

1. Weigh all the dry ingredients separately and place them into a large plastic bowl in the following order: flour first and then the salt, caster sugar, and milk powder in piles on top.

2. Thoroughly stir the ingredients together to fully disperse the milk powder and prevent any lumps from forming once the liquid is added.

3. Add the botanical culture, botanical water, and tap water, and combine until a dough starts to form and the sides of the bowl are clean. The dough will feel firm at this stage but will soften when the butter is added.

4. Remove the dough from the bowl and knead on a dry work surface until it becomes smooth and elastic, approximately 12 to 15 minutes.

5. Use the windowpane test (see page 36) to check if the dough is fully developed.

6. Place the dough back into your plastic bowl and add the butter. Using one hand, start squeezing the butter into the dough. It may take a little while but keep persevering.

7. After the butter is fully incorporated, place the dough on the work surface and knead until it feels smooth and elastic.

8. Flatten the dough, sprinkle a layer of currants, sultanas, and grated orange and lemon peel over the surface, roll up the dough, and gently knead to start evenly distributing them throughout the dough, trying not to damage the dried fruit too much, as the sugar within them will leach out into the dough and cause the tea cakes to bake very dark.

9. Divide the dough into eight 125 g (4^{1}/$_{3}$ ounce) pieces and gently shape them into round balls.

10. Place into a lidded plastic container and leave to bulk ferment for 30 minutes.

11. Remove the dough balls from the container and gently reshape.

12. Place back into the container for another 30 minutes.

13. Remove the dough balls from the container and once again gently reshape.

14. Place back into the container for another 10 minutes.

Continues...

355 g (12½ ounces) strong white bread flour

3.5 g (2 pinches) salt

45 g (1½ ounces) caster sugar

10 g (⅓ ounce) milk powder

150 g (5¼ ounces) currants, sultanas, and Earl Grey tea botanical culture

170 g (6 ounces) currants, sultanas, and Earl Grey tea botanical water

70 g (2½ ounces) softened unsalted butter

100 g (3½ ounces) currants (washed and drained)

100 g (3½ ounces) sultanas (washed and drained)

20 g (⅔ ounce) freshly grated orange and lemon peel

Beaten egg, for brushing over the top (optional)

FLOUR HYDRATION LEVEL (PERCENTAGE WATER TO FLOUR):

Recipe provides 56.9 percent hydration.

CURRANTS, SULTANAS, AND EARL GREY TEA FERMENT:

To build my ferment, I use good-quality currants and sultanas and Earl Grey tea leaves. Place the currants, sultanas, and Earl Grey tea leaves into a fermenting jar, cover them with water, and close the lid. This will usually ferment quickly due to the sugars within the currants and sultanas. The fermenting liquid also makes a lovely refreshing drink; combine half currants, sultanas, and Earl Grey tea botanical water and half chilled sparkling water.

TIP:

When using a rolling pin on the dough, always roll from the middle outward/middle backward, give a quarter turn, and then roll again middle outward/middle backward. Keep this going and the dough will stretch neater while you achieve the desired disk shape.

15. Remove the dough balls from the container and, using a rolling pin, gently roll them into approximately 5-inch (12.5 cm) disks.

16. Place each disk on a baking paper-lined baking tray. Make sure to leave enough space around each one for expansion while proving and baking, so that when fully baked, the buns are not fused together. This may require two trays.

17. Place the tray(s) into a large, lidded plastic storage box and leave to fully prove. This could take from 3 to 6 hours, depending on the activity of the ferment.

18. When fully proved, remove the tray(s) from the storage box. Before baking, as an option, brush the top surface with beaten egg, to impart a darker color to the top surface. Place into the oven and bake at 400°F (200°C, or gas mark 6) for 12 to 15 minutes until golden brown.

19. Remove the tray from the oven and place on a cooling rack.

Yield: 8 tea cakes

TIP:

The fermenting liquid also makes a refreshing drink; combine equal parts currants, sultanas, and Earl Grey tea botanical water and chilled sparkling water, and enjoy!

**FLOUR
HYDRATION LEVEL
(PERCENTAGE
WATER TO FLOUR):**

Recipe provides
56.3 percent hydration.

APPLE AND CLOVE BUNS

This is an ideal bake for those who grow their own apples. In this recipe, you can use your homegrown apples in the botanical ferment and for making the apple filling. A soft, fluffy sweet bun dough is filled with apple before proving and baking. When baked, the top is glazed to highlight the fresh apple filling. This is one of those simple products that is so divine when eaten, maybe with a nice pot of English breakfast tea too.

In addition to the Apple and Clove Buns, you will also need to make the Apple Filling recipe (see below). You could make this after step 7 in the recipe while waiting for the dough to bulk ferment. Alternatively, you could use a good-quality, store-bought pie filling.

Continues...

DOUGH:

355 g (12½ ounces) strong white bread flour

4 g (2 pinches) salt

35 g (1¼ ounces) caster sugar

10 g (⅓ ounce) milk powder

50 g (1¾ ounces) softened unsalted butter

10 g (⅓ ounce) egg yolk (at room temperature)

160 g (5¾ ounces) apple and clove botanical culture

160 g (5¾ ounces) apple and clove botanical water

Apricot jam, heated, for brushing on top

APPLE AND CLOVE FERMENT:

To build my ferment, I chop homegrown apples into quarters (or eighths if large) and use whole cloves. Place the chopped apple pieces and cloves into a fermenting jar, cover them with water, and close the lid. This will usually ferment quickly due to the sugars within the apples. The fermenting liquid also makes a lovely refreshing drink: combine half apple and clove botanical water and half chilled sparkling water.

1. Weigh all the dry ingredients separately and place them into a large plastic bowl in the following order: flour first and then the salt, caster sugar, and milk powder in separate piles on top.

2. Thoroughly stir the ingredients together to fully disperse the milk powder to prevent any lumps from forming once the liquid is added.

3. Add the softened butter, egg yolk, botanical culture, and botanical water and combine until a dough starts to form and the sides of the bowl are clean.

4. Remove the dough from the bowl and knead on a dry work surface until it becomes smooth and elastic, approximately 12 to 15 minutes. Expect the dough to feel firm but slightly sticky for the first few minutes of the kneading process.

5. Use the windowpane test (see page 36) to check if the dough is fully developed.

6. Divide the dough into ten 75 g (2¾ ounce) pieces and gently shape into ball shapes.

7. Place into a lidded plastic container and leave to bulk ferment for 30 minutes.

8. Remove the dough balls from the container and gently reshape.

9. Place back into the container for another 30 minutes.

10. Remove the dough balls from the container and once again gently reshape.

11. Place back into the container for another 10 minutes.

12. Remove the dough balls from the container and, using a piece of doweling, insert the stick down through the top center of each one and wiggle it to make a cavity big enough to fill with a dollop of your Apple Filling.

13. Place each piece on a baking paper-lined baking tray. Make sure to leave enough space around each one for expansion while proving and baking, so that when fully baked, the buns are not fused together. This may require two trays.

14. Fill each dough piece with a dollop of Apple Filling.

15. Place the tray into a large, lidded plastic storage box and leave to prove. This could take from 3 to 6 hours, depending on the activity of the ferment.

16. When nearly fully proved, press back in the escaping Apple Filling.

17. Remove the tray from the storage box and bake in an oven preheated to 400°F (200°C, or gas mark 6) for 10 to 12 minutes. The buns will be golden brown and will soften as they cool.

18. Remove the tray from the oven and place on a cooling rack.

19. When cool, brush the top of each bun with apricot jam. This will give a nice shine to the baked buns and also keep the Apple Filling moist and soft to eat.

Yield: 10 buns

APPLE FILLING:

I like to use Bramley apples for this recipe, but you can replace them with your favorite variety or your own homegrown apples. You can also adjust the sugar quantity to change the sweetness if using different apples. You could also mix in some spices, such as ground cloves or cinnamon.

Juice of 1 large lemon

70 g (2¹/2 ounces) tap water

255 g (9 ounces) caster sugar

4 large Bramley apples

Cornstarch (10 percent of the weight of the drained liquid once the apples have been cooked.)

1. Place the lemon juice, water, and sugar into a saucepan and bring to a boil and then a simmer.

2. While the saucepan is heating, start peeling and slicing the apples. Add the apples immediately to the hot liquid to prevent them from browning.

3. Gently stir the apples as they cook because some may not be completely submerged in the liquid.

4. Cook until the slices are softened but still slightly crisp.

5. Remove from the heat and drain—but don't throw out—the liquid.

6. Gently pour the apples onto a flat tray to cool.

7. Weigh the drained liquid. Place 90 percent of it back into the pan.

8. Thoroughly mix the remaining 10 percent of liquid with the same weight of cornstarch until there are no lumps.

9. Pour the liquid cornstarch mixture into the liquid from the cooked apples and bring to a boil, stirring continuously with a whisk to produce a smooth, thick sauce.

10. Place the cooked apples into a bowl, pour the thickened cooked apple liquid over them, and gently fold through until evenly dispersed.

11. Cover the bowl and leave to cool.

12. When cool, store in the refrigerator until needed. This will keep for 2 weeks in the fridge.

ORANGE AND MADAGASCAR VANILLA PANETTONE

310 g (11 ounces) strong white bread flour

2 g (pinch) salt

10 g ($^1/_3$ ounce) milk powder

40 g (1$^1/_3$ ounces) caster sugar

50 g (1$^3/_4$ ounces) egg yolk (at room temperature)

Vanilla extract (to taste)

100 g (3$^1/_2$ ounces) orange and Madagascar vanilla botanical culture

This recipe makes eight fresh, light, and airy citrus panettone, which are unbelievably moist too. These little beauties are far more enjoyable to eat compared to the long-life ones you find in the extravagant tins and boxes. You will need eight paper cases or ramekins about 3 inches (7.5 cm) in diameter. The dough will start off as a slightly firm but sticky dough and then turn to a silky-smooth soft dough once the butter has been fully incorporated.

1. Weigh all the dry ingredients separately and place them into a large plastic bowl in the following order: flour first and then the salt, milk powder, and caster sugar in separate piles on top.

2. Thoroughly stir the ingredients together to fully disperse the milk powder and prevent any lumps from forming once the liquid is added.

3. Add the egg yolk, vanilla, botanical culture, and botanical water and combine until a dough starts to form and the sides of the bowl are clean.

4. Remove the dough from the bowl and knead on a dry work surface until the dough becomes smooth. Although the dough is slightly firm, it will feel sticky too, due to the sugar.

5. Gently shape the dough into a round ball.

6. Place into a plastic bowl, cover with plastic wrap or a clean, plastic shower cap, and leave to bulk ferment for 30 minutes.

7. Remove the cover from the bowl, add the softened butter, and start to combine the dough and butter together. It will take a while but persevere as it will eventually get there.

8. After the butter is fully incorporated, place the very soft dough on a work surface and knead, using the slap-and-fold method (see page 34), until it feels smooth and elastic.

9. Use the windowpane test (see page 36) to check if the dough is fully developed. It should feel soft but silky smooth.

10. Gently shape the dough into a round ball.

11. Place into a plastic bowl, cover with plastic wrap or a clean, plastic shower cap, and leave to bulk ferment for another 30 minutes.

12. Add the sultanas and grated orange peel to the dough in the plastic bowl after its second 30-minute bulk fermentation.

13. Gently knead the ingredients into the dough until thoroughly blended in.

14. Divide the dough into eight 110 g (4 ounce) pieces and gently shape them into round balls.

15. Place the dough balls into a lidded plastic container to rest for 20 minutes.

16. Remove the dough balls from the container and gently reshape.

130 g (4¹/₂ ounces) orange and Madagascar vanilla botanical water

130 g (4¹/₂ ounces) softened unsalted butter

150 g (5¹/₄ ounces) sultanas (washed and drained)

20 g (²/₃ ounce) grated orange peel

White vegetable shortening, for greasing ramekins (optional)

Beaten egg, for brushing over the top

Sliced almonds, for decoration

ORANGE AND MADAGASCAR VANILLA FERMENT:

To build my ferment, I chop navel oranges into quarters and add a couple of Madagascar vanilla pods cut into thirds. Place the oranges and vanilla pods into a fermenting jar, cover them with water, and close the lid. This will usually ferment quickly due to the sugars within the oranges. The fermenting liquid also makes a lovely refreshing drink; combine half orange and Madagascar vanilla botanical water and half chilled sparkling water.

FLOUR HYDRATION LEVEL (PERCENTAGE WATER TO FLOUR):

Recipe provides 56.9 percent hydration.

17. Place into your panettone paper cases or lightly greased ramekins of approximately 3 inches (7.5 cm) in diameter with the smooth side of the dough facing up.

18. Place the cases or ramekins onto a baking tray and into a large, lidded plastic storage box and leave to fully prove for at least 6 hours or more. They should expand two to three times their original size.

19. When fully proved, gently brush the top of each ball of dough with beaten eggs and sprinkle on a few sliced almonds.

20. Place the tray in the preheated oven and bake at 350°F (180°C, or gas mark 4) until a rich golden-brown color, approximately 15 to 20 minutes.

21. Remove the baked panettone from the oven and place on a cooling rack.

Yield: 8 small panettone

CHOCOLATE ORANGE BRIOCHE

325 g (11½ ounces) strong white bread flour	40 g (1⅓ ounces) egg yolk (at room temperature)	120 g (4¼ ounces) softened unsalted butter
4 g (2 pinches) salt	150 g (5¼ ounces) navel orange botanical culture	100 g (3½ ounces) dark chocolate chips (optional)
32 g (1 ounce) caster sugar		
10 g (⅓ ounce) milk powder	135 g (4¾ ounces) navel orange botanical water	

Brioche is a traditional sweet fermented dough that is extremely rich in butter and eggs, producing a silky-smooth melt-in-the-mouth sensation. This recipe has chocolate chips included to complement the orange flavor. I recommend using Belgian dark chocolate, as this delivers the richest chocolate taste.

This recipe requires two small bread pans, lined with baking paper.

1. Weigh all the dry ingredients separately and place them into a large plastic bowl in the following order: flour first and then the salt, caster sugar, and milk powder in separate piles on top.

2. Thoroughly stir the ingredients together to fully disperse the milk powder and prevent any lumps from forming once the liquid is added.

3. Add the egg yolk, botanical culture, and botanical water and combine until a dough starts to form and the sides of the bowl are clean.

4. Remove the dough from the bowl and knead on a dry work surface until it becomes smooth and elastic, approximately 12 to 15 minutes. Expect the dough to feel firm but slightly sticky as you knead. After the butter is added, the dough will soften.

5. Use the windowpane test (see page 36) to check if the dough is fully developed.

6. Place the dough back in your plastic bowl and add the butter. Using one hand, start squeezing the butter into the dough. It may take a little while but keep persevering.

7. After the butter is fully incorporated, place the very soft dough on a work surface and knead, using the slap-and-fold method (see page 34), until it feels smooth and elastic. It may take a while, but persevere as it will eventually get there. For a second time, use the windowpane test to check if the dough is fully developed.

8. Flatten the dough, sprinkle a layer of chocolate chips over the surface, roll up the dough, and gently knead to evenly distribute the chocolate within the dough. Try not to be too heavy-handed, as it will cause the dough to stain a gray color from the chocolate.

9. Divide the dough into two 450 g (1 pound) pieces and gently shape them into round balls. (If you do not choose to add chocolate chips, the dough pieces will weigh 400 g [14 ounces] each.)

10. Place the dough balls into a lidded plastic container and leave to bulk ferment for 45 minutes.

11. Remove the dough balls from the container and gently reshape.

12. Place back into the container for another 45 minutes.

13. Remove the dough balls from the container and once again gently reshape.

14. Place back into the container for another 10 minutes.

15. Remove the dough balls from the container and form them into cylindrical

NAVEL ORANGE FERMENT:

To build my ferment, I chop navel oranges into quarters. Place the orange quarters into a fermenting jar, cover them with water, and close the lid. This will usually ferment quickly due to the sugars within the oranges.

TIP:

Have a plastic bowl scraper handy when working with the soft dough on the table. You will find this useful to gather up the dough as you are working with it, until the dough becomes more bound together. You will find it ideal for scraping your hands clean too!

TIP:

The fermenting liquid also makes a lovely refreshing drink; combine equal parts navel orange botanical water and chilled sparkling water, and enjoy.

FLOUR HYDRATION LEVEL (PERCENTAGE WATER TO FLOUR):

Recipe provides 57.5 percent hydration.

shapes the length of the loaf pan being used. Line the pans with baking paper; otherwise, the chocolate will burn against the inside of the pan.

16. Place the loaf pans into a large, lidded plastic storage box to fully prove. This could take from 3 to 6 hours, depending on the activity of the ferment.

17. When fully proved, remove the pans from the storage box, place into the preheaetd oven, and bake at 400°F (200°C, or gas mark 7) for approximately 20 minutes. The brioche loaves should be dark brown on top and golden on the sides.

18. Allow the brioche to cool in the pans for 30 minutes before removing.

Yield: 2 small brioche loaves

FIG AND HAZELNUT STAR

325 g (11½ ounces) strong white bread flour	10 g (⅓ ounce) milk powder
4 g (2 pinches) salt	40 g (1⅓ ounces) egg yolk (at room temperature)
32 g (1 ounce) caster sugar	150 g (5¼ ounces) fig and hazelnut botanical culture

This breakfast centerpiece is based on a brioche-style dough, which is extremely rich in butter and eggs, and then layered with copious amounts of chocolate hazelnut spread. You will be able to wow your friends and family with this heavenly beauty. It is great fun to make; try to avoid getting covered in chocolate hazelnut spread or licking your fingers when you do. If eaten while still hot, it is extremely difficult not to return for a second helping. My advice is . . . double the recipe and make two!

1. Weigh all the dry ingredients separately and place them into a large plastic bowl in the following order: flour first and then the salt, caster sugar, and milk powder in separate piles on top.

2. Thoroughly stir the ingredients together to fully disperse the milk powder and prevent any lumps from forming once the liquid is added.

3. Add the egg yolk, botanical culture, and botanical water and combine until a dough starts to form and the sides of the bowl are clean.

4. Remove the dough from the bowl and knead on a dry work surface until it becomes smooth and elastic, approximately 12 to 15 minutes. Expect the dough to feel firm but slightly sticky as you knead. After the butter is added, the dough will soften.

5. Use the windowpane test (see page 36) to check if the dough is fully developed.

6. Place the dough back into the plastic bowl and add the butter. Using one hand, start squeezing the butter into the dough. It may take a little while but keep persevering.

7. After the butter is fully incorporated, place the very soft dough on the work surface and knead, using the slap-and-fold method (see page 34), until it feels smooth and elastic. This may take a while. For a second time, use the windowpane test to check if the dough is fully developed.

8. Divide the dough into three 265 g (9⅓ ounce) pieces and gently shape them into round balls.

9. Place the dough balls into a lidded plastic container and leave to bulk ferment for 45 minutes.

10. Remove the dough balls from the container and gently reshape.

11. Place back into the container for another 45 minutes.

12. Remove the dough balls from the container and once again gently reshape.

13. Place back into the container for another 10 minutes.

14. Remove the dough balls from the container and, using a rolling pin, shape the dough to form three 10-inch (25.5 cm) round disks. You will need to lightly dust the table and dough with flour to prevent it from sticking.

Continues...

135 g (4³/₄ ounces) fig and hazelnut botanical water

120 g (4¹/₄ ounces) softened unsalted butter

Flour, for dusting

Large jar of chocolate hazelnut spread (place jar in hot water to gently warm if too hard to spread)

Beaten eggs, for brushing over the top

FIG AND HAZELNUT FERMENT:

To build my ferment, I use fresh figs cut in half or quarters (depending on the size) and whole hazelnuts. Place the cut figs and hazelnuts into a fermenting jar, cover them with water, and close the lid. This will usually ferment quickly due to the sugars within the figs.

FLOUR HYDRATION LEVEL (PERCENTAGE WATER TO FLOUR):

Recipe provides 57.5 percent hydration.

Have a plastic bowl scraper at hand when working with the soft buttery dough on the table. You will find this useful to gather up the dough as you are working with it, until the dough becomes more bound together. You will also find it ideal for scraping your hands clean too!

15. Place one disk on a baking paper-lined baking tray and spread on a layer of chocolate hazelnut spread, leaving the outer edge free from any topping.

16. Carefully place a second disk over the top, trying to keep the round shape.

17. Spread more chocolate hazelnut spread over this second disk of dough.

18. Finally, place the remaining disk on top and gently form the sides into a neat round shape.

19. Carefully, using the back of a long knife, mark the top surface into 16 equal portions (do not cut through the layers).

20. Place the tray into a large, lidded plastic storage box to prove until half proved, approximately 2 to 3 hours.

21. Remove the tray from the storage box and, using a pizza wheel, cut along all the 16 lines, starting from the outer edge and finishing 2 inches (5 cm) from the middle.

22. Hold the ends of two strips of dough (next to each other) and twist them simultaneously toward each other three times. Pinch the ends together to form a point. Repeat this all the way around to form an eight-pointed star.

23. Place back into to the storage box to continue proving, approximately another 2 to 3 hours.

24. When fully proved, remove the tray from the storage box, brush the top surface with beaten egg, place into the preheated oven, and bake at 400°F (200°C, or gas mark 6) for approximately 12 to 15 minutes. The brioche should be golden brown on top and lightly golden on the sides. Try not to overbake.

25. Once baked, remove from the oven and leave to cool a little on the tray before devouring!

Yield: 1 star

ORANGE, LEMON, LICORICE STICK, AND STREGA LIQUEUR SAVARIN AND RUM BABA

DOUGH:

400 g (14 ounces) strong white bread flour	85 g (3 ounces) egg yolk (at room temperature)	290 g (10¼ ounces) orange, lemon and licorice stick botanical water	Apricot jam, for glazing
40 g (1⅓ ounces) caster sugar	200 g (7 ounces) orange, lemon and licorice stick botanical culture	White vegetable shortening, for greasing pans	
120 g (4¼ ounces) softened unsalted butter			

This recipe creates a rich, buttery, soft dough. Once baked, each piece is soaked—more like *drenched*—in a sugar syrup, creating a distinctive "refreshing" eating experience. In this recipe, I have incorporated the popular Italian liqueur Strega. This liqueur has a licorice flavor and aroma, which makes a pleasant addition to Italian pastries and desserts.

You can replace the Strega with other liqueurs if preferred: Grand Marnier or Limoncello, for example. Alternatively, replace the alcohol with a couple of licorice or cinnamon sticks instead.

You will need some rum baba or savarin cake pans to bake the batter in. Rum babas and savarins differ visually by the shape of the pan they are baked in. Rum babas are shaped like a champagne cork; therefore, it is possible to use cupcake pans as an alternative to rum baba pans. However, savarins are shaped like a ring donut or a small Bundt cake. Whichever pans you use, make sure they are well greased before adding the batter.

After the savarins or rum babas soak in a syrup, they are glazed with apricot jam. This helps keep them moist inside, and the imparted shine makes them more attractive. Once glazed, serve the rum babas as they are. The savarins can be decorated with some whipped cream and fresh berries in the middle.

1. Weigh the dry ingredients separately and place them into a large plastic bowl in the following order: flour first and then the sugar. You can carry out all the mixing in a stand mixer with a beater attachment.

2. Add the softened butter and mix until a crumble is formed.

3. Add the egg yolk, botanical culture, and half of the botanical water and mix until a lump-free paste is formed. Scrape down the bowl.

4. Stream in the remaining half of the botanical water, scrape down the bowl, and mix for a couple of minutes to produce a smooth batter.

5. Cover the bowl with plastic wrap or a clean, plastic shower cap and leave for an hour.

6. The batter is now ready for filling your baking pans. I find it much easier to use a piping bag to fill my baking pans. The cupcake pans contain 60 g (2 ounces) and the 4¼-inch (11.5 cm) Bundt cake pans contain 110 g (4 ounces). Whatever pan size you use, fill them three-quarters full of the batter.

7. Place the baking pans into a large, lidded plastic storage box to fully prove. This could take from 3 to 6 hours,

ORANGE, LEMON, AND LICORICE STICK FERMENT:

To build my ferment, I chop oranges and lemons into quarters and break the licorice sticks in half or thirds, depending on the length of them. Place the orange and lemon quarters and licorice sticks into a fermenting jar, cover them with water, and close the lid. This will usually ferment quickly due to the sugars within the oranges and lemons.

depending on the activity of the ferment. The batter should expand to protrude to the top of the pans.

8. When fully proved, remove the pans from the storage box, place into the preheated oven, and bake at 350°F (180°C, or gas mark 4) for approximately 12 to 15 minutes for the cupcake-size pans and 15 to 18 minutes for the larger Bundt cake–size pans. The rum babas or savarins should be golden brown and bulbous.

9. Allow to cool in the pan for 30 minutes before carefully removing from the pans.

10. When cool, place the baked rum babas or savarins, one at a time, in the bowl of Strega Liqueur Syrup or Spiced Savarin/Rum Baba Syrup and turn to absorb the liquid. Approximately a minute is generally enough soaking time. As you remove each one, let the excess syrup run back into the bowl. Place on a cooling rack to allow any further syrup to run off.

11. Boil some apricot jam in a saucepan and generously brush each rum baba or savarin with the jam. If the jam is thick, add some water to bring it to a consistency that does not retain the brush marks.

Yield: Will vary depending upon the size of the pans used

TIP:

Make the syrup the day before to allow the ingredients to infuse, generating increased flavor in the syrup.

TIP:

The fermenting liquid also makes a refreshing drink; combine equal parts orange, lemon, and licorice stick botanical water and chilled sparkling water, and enjoy.

STREGA LIQUEUR SYRUP:

1250 g (2 pounds 12 ounces) tap water

500 g (1 pound 1½ ounces) caster sugar

85 g (3 ounces) Strega liqueur

1. In a large saucepan, boil together the tap water and sugar for a few minutes.

2. Remove from the heat and leave to cool.

3. Add the Strega and stir through. Taste and add more if preferred.

SPICED SAVARIN/ RUM BABA SYRUP:

1250 g (2 pounds 12 ounces) tap water

500 g (1 pound 1½ ounces) caster sugar

1 large orange, zest and juice

1 large lemon, zest and juice

1 bay leaf

2 cinnamon sticks

1. In a large saucepan, boil together all the ingredients for a few minutes.

2. Remove from the heat and leave to cool.

AWARD-WINNING PECAN AND RAISIN RICKY STICKY BUNS

These awesome sticky buns evolved from our award-winning Cinnamon Square Buns and are named after my hometown of Rickmansworth, England. This product has become a real winner, literally! It won the specialty category at the World Bread Awards. These sweet fermented buns are rolled with a cinnamon filling and finished with a sticky caramelized pecan topping: the Ricky Sticky Goo.

Although these buns are lovely to eat at room temperature, I recommend eating them warm, either soon after they exit the oven or reheated in the microwave so they stay all soft and gooey.

This recipe requires a 9-inch (23 cm) square baking pan.

1. Weigh all the dry ingredients separately and place them into a large plastic bowl in the following order: flour first and then the caster sugar, salt, and milk powder in separate piles on top.

2. Thoroughly stir the ingredients together to fully disperse the milk powder to prevent any lumps from forming once the liquid is added.

3. Add the botanical culture, botanical water, and tap water, and combine until a dough starts to form and the sides of the bowl are clean.

4. Remove the dough from the bowl and knead on your work surface until it becomes smooth and elastic, approximately 12 to 15 minutes. Expect the dough to feel firm as you knead. When the butter is added, it will then become soft.

5. Use the windowpane test (see page 36) to check if the dough is fully developed.

6. Place the dough back into the plastic bowl and add the butter. Using one hand, start squeezing the butter into the dough. It may take a little while but keep persevering.

7. After the butter is fully incorporated, place the dough on a dry work surface and knead until it feels smooth and elastic.

8. Form the dough into a cylindrical shape.

9. Place the dough into a lidded plastic container and leave to bulk ferment for 30 minutes.

10. Remove the dough from the container and gently reshape it into a rectangle.

11. Place back into the container for another 30 minutes.

12. Remove the dough from the container and, using a rolling pin, roll the dough into an 8 x 14-inch (20 x 35.5 cm) rectangle.

13. Rotate the dough so the 8-inch (20 cm) edge is closest to you.

14. Using a pallet knife, spread the Ricky Sticky Bun Filling over the dough, leaving the edge closest to you free from any filling.

15. Press flat the edge closest to you and lightly spray with water.

16. Starting from the end furthest from you, roll the dough into an 8-inch (20 cm)-long cylindrical shape of uniform thickness.

Continues...

DOUGH:

250 g (8³/₄ ounces) strong white bread flour

25 g (1 ounce) caster sugar

3 g (pinch) salt

10 g (¹/₃ ounce) milk powder

100 g (3¹/₂ ounces) pecan and raisin botanical culture

120 g (4¹/₄ ounces) pecan and raisin botanical water

25 g (1 ounce) softened unsalted butter

FLOUR HYDRATION LEVEL (PERCENTAGE WATER TO FLOUR):

Recipe provides 56.6 percent hydration.

PECAN AND RAISIN FERMENT:

To build my ferment, I use whole or broken pecans and good-quality, ready-to-eat raisins. Place the pecans and the raisins into a fermenting jar, cover them with water, and close the lid. This will usually ferment quickly due to the sugars within the raisins.

17. Using a long, sharp serrated knife, cut four 2-inch (5 cm) buns. Use a sawing motion to prevent squashing the rolled dough pieces.

18. Place the buns, swirl-side up, into a baking paper-lined 9-inch (23 cm) square baking pan.

19. Place the baking pan into a large, lidded plastic storage box to fully prove. This could take from 3 to 6 hours, depending on the activity of the ferment.

20. When fully proved, remove from the storage box, spoon a dollop of the Ricky Sticky Goo on top, and bake in the preheated oven at 400°F (200°C, or gas mark 6) for 10 to 12 minutes.

21. Remove the tray from the oven and place on a cooling rack.

22. They are now ready to eat, warm and gooey!

Caution! The Ricky Sticky Goo may overflow the baking pan onto the tray. Do not touch the glaze directly after baking, as it will be extremely hot!

Yield: 4 buns

RICKY STICKY BUN FILLING:

100 g (3^{1}/2 ounces) caster sugar

50 g (1^{3}/4 ounces) softened unsalted butter

10 g (^{1}/3 ounce) ground cinnamon

Combine the ingredients in a bowl with a spoon until thoroughly mixed together.

RICKY STICKY GOO:

50 g (1^{3}/4 ounces) unsalted butter

25 g (1 ounce) honey

25 g (1 ounce) glucose syrup (or corn syrup)

100 g (3^{1}/2 ounces) demerara sugar

75 g (2^{3}/4 ounces) pecan pieces

Melt the butter in a bowl in the microwave, add the remaining ingredients, and stir together with a spoon until thoroughly combined.

WILLIAMS PEAR AND CARDAMOM BUNS

FLOUR HYDRATION LEVEL (PERCENTAGE WATER TO FLOUR):

Recipe provides 567 percent hydration.

Continues...

DOUGH:

250 g (8³/₄ ounces) strong white bread flour

3 g (pinch) salt

10 g (¹/₃ ounce) milk powder

120 g (4¹/₄ ounces) pear and cardamom botanical water

Beaten egg, for brushing over the top

25 g (1 ounce) caster sugar

100 g (3¹/₂ ounces) pear and cardamom botanical culture

25 g (1 ounce) softened unsalted butter

The spice cardamom is a common ingredient in Turkish and Indian cooking. I always add cardamom pods to my rice when I try my hand at making curries, as they add a wonderful aromatic infusion. Spiced cardamom buns, as well as cinnamon buns, are a huge Nordic favorite. Although cardamom has a powerful flavor and aroma, the sweetness of this botanical bun dough balances out the intense cardamom spice to form a harmonious sweet roll that is a wonderful example of this Scandinavian classic.

1. Weigh all the dry ingredients separately and place them into a large plastic bowl in the following order: flour first and then the caster sugar, salt, and milk powder in separate piles on top.

2. Thoroughly stir the ingredients together to fully disperse the milk powder and prevent any lumps from forming once the liquid is added.

3. Add the botanical culture, botanical water, and tap water, and combine until a dough starts to form and the sides of the bowl are clean.

4. Remove the dough from the bowl and knead on a dry work surface until it becomes smooth and elastic, approximately 12 to 15 minutes. Expect the dough to feel firm as you knead. When the butter is added, the dough will soften.

5. Use the windowpane test (see page 36) to check if the dough is fully developed.

6. Place the dough back into the plastic bowl and add the butter. Using one hand, start squeezing the butter into the dough. It may take a little while but keep persevering.

10

7. After the butter is fully incorporated, place the dough on the work surface and knead until it feels smooth and elastic.

8. Form the dough into a cylindrical shape.

9. Place the dough into a lidded plastic container and leave to bulk ferment for 30 minutes.

10. Remove the dough from the container and gently reshape the dough into a rectangle.

11. Place back into the container for another 30 minutes.

12. Remove the dough from the container and, using a rolling pin, roll the dough into a 24 x 9½-inch (60 x 48 cm) rectangle.

13. Rotate the dough so the 9½-inch (24 cm) edge is closest to you.

14. Using a pallet knife, spread the Cardamom Bun Filling over the top 12 inches (30 cm) of dough, leaving the half closest to you free from any filling.

15. Fold the unfilled half upward to cover the cardamom-filled half; the rectangle will now measure 12 x 9½ inches (30 x 24 cm).

16. Using a pizza wheel, cut six 1½-inch (4 cm)-wide vertical strips.

17. Carefully cut the six strips vertically in half to create twelve ¾-inch (2 cm)-wide strips.

18. Cut across horizontally to divide the twelve strips in half to give two rows of twelve strips measuring ¾ x 6 inches (2 x 15 cm).

19. Leave the dough strips for a couple of minutes to let them relax.

Continues...

20. Taking two sets of dough strips in pairs (one pair from the top row and one pair from the bottom row), gently stretch them to make them longer. This will help make the shaping easier. Place the dough pairs in a cross as shown in the photographs. Now, carefully follow the shaping directions in the photos.

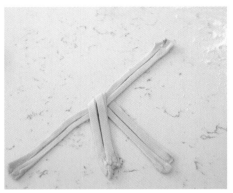

PEAR AND CARDAMOM FERMENT:

To build my ferment, I use organic Williams pears, often called Bartlett pears in the United States, cut into quarters and use whole cardamom pods. Place the pears and the cardamom pods into a fermenting jar, cover them with water, and close the lid. This will usually ferment quickly due to the sugars within the pears.

21. Place the shaped cardamom bun on a baking paper–lined baking tray.

22. Repeat this shaping with the remaining pairs of dough to end up with 6 cardamom buns.

23. Place the tray into a large, lidded plastic storage box to fully prove. This could take from 3 to 6 hours, depending on the activity of your ferment.

24. When fully proved, remove from the storage box, brush the tops with beaten egg, and bake in the preheated oven at 400°F (200°C, or gas mark 6) for 8 to 10 minutes.

25. Remove the tray from the oven, generously brush Medium Sugar Syrup over each bun, and leave on the tray to cool.

Yield: 6 buns

TIP:

Add a few cardamom pods to the sugar syrup. These will infuse in the syrup and impart more flavor to the bun.

CARDAMOM BUN FILLING:

7 g (¼ ounce) whole cardamom pods

100 g (3½ ounces) caster sugar

50 g (1¾ ounces) softened unsalted butter

1. Using a mortar and pestle, crush the cardamom pods.

2. Place the sugar, butter, and ground cardamom in a bowl and combine thoroughly using a wooden spoon.

MEDIUM SUGAR SYRUP:

100 g (3½ ounces) caster sugar

200 g (7 ounces) tap water

1. Place the sugar and tap water into a saucepan and gently boil for a couple of minutes.

2. Leave to cool. Store any remaining syrup in the fridge.

CHAPTER 5

SOURDOUGH BREADS

The most wonderful flavors, aromas, and textures can be found in baked sourdough loaves. These attributes arise from a simple mixture of flour and water and the baker's understanding of how to nurture these qualities.

At Cinnamon Square, I started our own sour cultures in 2005: one wheat based and the other rye. In 2010, we won a Great Taste Gold Award for our Wheat and Rye Sourdough, and in 2017, our Church Street Sourdough was awarded the best loaf in the United Kingdom at the British Baking Industry Awards. I will share both recipes with you in this chapter.

Sourdough can be considered another form of baking botanically and, therefore, has a place in this book, as the sour culture itself is made from fermented cereals: generally, wheat or rye flours. For sourdoughs, the flour/water mixture is purposely left to sour, and the resulting culture is then regularly fed with more flour and water. If regularly maintained, a mature sour culture will last indefinitely, whereas a botanical fermentation is generally only used for a few weeks while the flavors are clean and fresh.

To make your own sour culture, combine equal quantities of organic flour and water (for example, 50 g [1³/₄ ounces] of each), and mix to form a paste. Continue to feed the starter daily with half its weight of flour and half its weight of water. Basically, it's the same process as when making a botanical culture. Continue daily feeding and diskard when necessary to keep the total weight to a usable amount.

When the culture smells acidic and looks bubbly 4 to 6 hours after feeding, it is stable and ready for many years of baking ahead. You now are ready to make your first sourdough loaf.

Some recipes call for a rye sour culture. If you do not have a rye sour, you can easily make one by taking a piece of your existing wheat sour and feeding this portion daily with rye flour. After a few feeds, it will be predominantly rye and ready to use.

More detailed instructions for starting and maintaining a sour culture can be found on my website.

www.cinnamonsquare.com

EVERYDAY WHEAT SOURDOUGH

485 g (17 ounces) strong white bread flour

10 g (1/3 ounce) salt

195 g (7 ounces) wheat sour culture (100 percent hydration: fed twice daily for 3 days)

275 g (9 3/4 ounces) tap water (tepid)

Flour, for dusting

Ground rice or semolina, for dusting

This is the perfect recipe to start making your first sourdough bread at home. You will need a couple of bannetons or cane proving baskets or you can use a pair of small bread loaf pans instead. Make sure your sour culture is fully active before you make the dough to be sure that the bread will rise. I use this recipe at home to make all types of everyday white bread such as split tin loaves, bloomer breads, and farmhouse loaves.

The dough is not as soft as many other sourdoughs; therefore, it will be easier to handle. If you need to change the consistency of the dough, simply reduce or increase the water content.

1. Weigh the dry ingredients separately and place them into a large plastic bowl in the following order: flour first and then the salt.

2. Add the wheat sour culture and tap water and combine until a dough starts to form and the sides of the bowl are clean.

3. Remove the dough from the bowl and knead on a dry work surface until it becomes smooth and elastic, approximately 15 minutes.

4. Use the windowpane test (see page 36) to check if the dough is fully developed.

5. Divide the dough into two 475 g (1 pound 3/4 ounce) pieces and gently shape into round balls.

6. Place the dough balls into a lidded plastic container and leave to bulk ferment for 45 minutes.

7. Remove the dough balls from the container and gently reshape.

8. Place back into the container for another 45 minutes.

9. Remove the dough balls from the container and once again gently reshape.

10. Place back into the container for another 45 minutes.

11. Remove the dough balls from the container and once again gently reshape.

12. Place the dough balls directly into flour-dusted round proving baskets or form into cylindrical shapes and place into flour-dusted oblong proving baskets.

13. Place the baskets into a large, lidded plastic storage box and leave to fully prove. This could take from 3 to 6 hours, depending on the activity of the sour culture.

14. When fully proved, generously sprinkle some ground rice or semolina on a pizza peel or flat thin baking tray and then turn out the dough from the proving basket onto a prepared vessel of choice.

15. Score the dough surface using a very sharp knife or lame (see page 40).

16. Slide the dough onto your baking stone or heavy baking tray in an oven preheated to 425°F (220°C, or gas mark 7) and steam the oven (see page 43).

17. Bake until golden brown, approximately 30 minutes.

18. Remove the baked loaves from the oven and place on a cooling rack (if using loaf pans, remove the loaves from the pans to cool).

Yield: 2 small loaves

FLOUR HYDRATION LEVEL (PERCENTAGE WATER TO FLOUR):

Recipe provides
64 percent hydration.

Increase water to 310 g
(11 ounces) to achieve
70 percent hydration.

Increase water to 340 g
(12 ounces) to achieve
75 percent hydration.

Increase water to 370 g
(13 ounces) to achieve
80 percent hydration.

AWARD-WINNING CHURCH STREET SOUR

I developed this loaf as a tribute to the hometown of my bakery, Cinnamon Square in Rickmansworth, England. Its name comes from the street the bakery resides on, Church Street. The sour culture used within this bread was born in the shop in November 2005; therefore, it has strong provenance in the town.

The Church Street Sour is a moist, flavorful loaf and has an attractive floral appearance due to the special wrapping method detailed in the recipe below. The scored petal cuts obtain a crunchy finish and are great to break off and use with a dip for a snack.

When introduced, this loaf was received favorably by our customers and was subsequently bestowed the title of United Kingdom's best loaf at the 2017 Baking Industry Awards, which was a fantastic accolade from my peers in the baking industry. So, instead of keeping this under *lock and key*, I would like to share my recipe.

Chilling the dough after a three-quarter proof will make the task of scoring the dough simpler.

1. Weigh the dry ingredients separately and then place them into a large plastic bowl in the following order: the three flours first and then the salt.

2. Add the wheat sour culture and tap water and combine until a dough starts to form and the sides of the bowl are clean.

3. Remove the dough from the bowl and knead on a dry work surface until it becomes smooth and elastic, approximately 15 minutes.

4. Use the windowpane test (see page 36) to check if the dough is fully developed.

5. Divide the dough into two 350 g (12 1/2 ounce) pieces and two 130 g (3 1/2 ounce) pieces and gently shape into round balls.

6. Place the dough balls into a lidded plastic container and leave to bulk ferment for 30 minutes.

7. Remove the dough balls from the container and gently reshape.

8. Place back into the container for another 30 minutes.

9. Remove the dough balls from the container and once again gently reshape.

10. Place back into the container for another 30 minutes.

11. Remove the dough balls from the container and, using a rolling pin and flour to prevent sticking, gently roll out one of the smaller pieces of dough into an approximately 6-inch (15 cm) round disk. Brush the top generously with vegetable oil (leave the edges clear).

Continues...

380 g (13½ ounces) white bread flour

50 g (1¾ ounces) whole wheat bread flour

50 g (1¾ ounces) dark rye flour

10 g (⅓ ounce) salt

195 g (7 ounces) wheat sour culture (100 percent hydration: fed twice daily for 3 days)

300 g (10½ ounces) tap water

Flour, for dusting

Vegetable oil

Seeds of choice, for topping

Flour or ground rice, for dusting

FLOUR HYDRATION LEVEL (PERCENTAGE WATER TO FLOUR):

Recipe provides 68.8 percent hydration.

Increase water to 336 g (12 ounces) to achieve 75 percent hydration.

Increase water to 365 g (13 ounces) to achieve 80 percent hydration.

12. Take one of the larger balls of dough and gently reshape and then dip the top into a bowl of seeds.

13. Place the seeded top face down onto the oiled disk of dough and start to encase the ball of dough by pulling up from the unoiled edges. Repeat with the other large and small dough ball set.

14. Place the wrapped dough into a flour and ground rice-dusted proving basket with the collective folds facing upward and place into a large, lidded plastic storage box to reach three-quarter prove.

15. When three-quarter proved, turn out the dough onto a baker's peel covered with ground rice. Use a very sharp knife to carefully score the outer skin with 8 petal cuts (see page 40).

16. Place into a preheated oven, preferably on a baking stone, and bake at 425°F (220°C, or gas mark 7) for approximately 30 minutes.

Yield: 2 loaves

AWARD-WINNING WHEAT AND RYE SOURDOUGH

This bread is so nice it won a Great Taste Gold Award. When baked, the close-textured and tasty crumb make this such a versatile bread. Bake this loaf until it has a dark golden brown crust, as this brings out a delightful, slightly sweet, rye flavor.

You need to have an active rye sour culture prepared to make this bread. This is also a two-stage process, as you will make a rye biga, or preferment, the day before, which will be used as an ingredient in the dough the following day. The final dough has a firm consistency and should be proved on a baking tray rather than a cane proving basket, as it will not flow significantly during the long proving stage.

STAGE 1: RYE BIGA (PREPARE THE DAY BEFORE MAKING BREAD):

130 g (4^{1}/$_2$ ounces) dark rye flour

46 g (1^2/$_3$ ounces) dark rye sour culture (100 percent hydration: fed twice daily for 3 days)

72 g (2^1/$_2$ ounces) tap water

1. Add all the ingredients to a medium plastic bowl and, using a wooden spoon, stir until a thick, smooth paste is formed.

2. Cover the bowl with plastic wrap or a clean, plastic shower cap and leave at room temperature for up to 12 hours before use.

STAGE 2: FINAL DOUGH:

445 g (15^3/$_4$ ounces) strong white bread flour

12 g (^{1}/$_2$ ounce) salt

248 g (8^3/$_4$ ounces) rye biga (all of stage 1)

250 g (8^3/$_4$ ounces) tap water

Ground rice or semolina, for dusting

1. Weigh the dry ingredients separately and place them into a large plastic bowl in the following order: flour first and then the salt.

2. Add the rye biga and tap water and combine until a dough starts to form and the sides of the bowl are clean.

3. Remove the dough from the bowl and knead on a dry work surface until it becomes smooth and elastic, approximately 10 to 12 minutes.

4. Use the windowpane test (see page 36) to check if the dough is fully developed.

5. Gently shape the dough into a round ball.

6. Place into a lidded plastic container and leave to bulk ferment for 60 minutes.

7. Remove the dough from the container and gently reshape.

8. Place back into the container for another 60 minutes.

9. Remove the dough from container and once again gently reshape.

10. Place back into the container, smooth-side up, for 15 minutes to allow the dough to relax.

11. Gently reshape the dough and place smooth-side up on a baking paper–lined baking tray generously sprinkled with ground rice or semolina.

12. Place the tray into a large, lidded plastic storage box and leave to fully prove. This could take from 2 to 4 hours, depending on the activity of the sour culture, but it is normally quicker than for the wheat sourdough.

13. When fully proved, generously sprinkle some ground rice or semolina on a pizza peel or flat thin baking tray and then gently place the dough onto your prepared vessel of choice.

14. Cut a design on the top surface of the dough with a sharp knife or lame (see page 40).

15. Slide the dough onto your baking stone or heavy baking tray in an oven preheated to 425°F (220°C, or gas mark 7) and steam the oven (see page 43).

16. Bake until a dark, rich, golden-brown crust is formed, approximately 35 to 40 minutes.

17. Remove the baked loaf from the oven and place on a cooling rack.

Yield: 1 large loaf

FLOUR HYDRATION LEVEL (PERCENTAGE WATER TO FLOUR):

Recipe provides 58 percent hydration.

Increase final dough water to 294 g (10⅓ ounces) to achieve 65 percent hydration.

Increase final dough water to 324 g (11½ ounces) to achieve 70 percent hydration.

Increase final dough water to 354 g (12½ ounces) to achieve 75 percent hydration.

100 PERCENT DARK RYE SOURDOUGH BOULE

This recipe makes an authentic version of the classic dark rye loaf. Normally cut into thin slices when eaten, the bread has a sweet, tangy rye flavor, and the crumb has a slight stickiness to it. The appearance is fantastic as the dough expands and heavy cracks appear across the flour-dusted top.

This recipe requires a rye sour culture to leaven the dough. If you do not have one, the easiest way to convert a portion of your existing wheat sour culture is to feed it daily with rye flour. After a few days, it will look totally different as the wheat flour becomes ever more diluted.

Although this bread is a three-stage process, the steps are not very time-consuming.

STAGE 1: OVERNIGHT FERMENT:

55 g (2 ounces) dark rye sour culture (100 percent hydration: fed twice daily for 3 days)

530 g (1 pound 2³/4 ounces) tap water

185 g (6¹/2 ounces) dark rye flour

1. Place the rye sour culture, tap water, and dark rye flour into a bowl and mix together until it forms a runny batter free from any lumps.

2. Cover the bowl with plastic wrap or a clean, plastic shower cap and leave overnight to ferment in a cool place.

STAGE 2: FLOUR ADDITION AND BULK FERMENT:

155 g (5¹/2 ounces) dark rye flour

1. Add the dark rye flour to the overnight ferment and mix until thoroughly dispersed. This should have the consistency of toothpaste. If it is too soft, add a little bit more flour. The consistency is determined by the water absorption of the flour.

2. Cover the bowl and leave to ferment for 2 to 4 hours. It should double in size.

STAGE 3: FINAL DOUGH:

285 g (10 ounces) dark rye flour, plus more for dusting

15 g (¹/2 ounce) salt

1. Mix together the dark rye flour and salt in a small bowl and add them to the ferment from stage 2. Mix thoroughly by hand for a few minutes. This will be a soft, nonelastic dough and very sticky on your hands. If you prefer, you can use a stand mixer with a beater attachment instead.

2. Place the dough back into the bowl, cover, and leave it for 45 minutes.

3. Stir the dough for about 20 seconds to help build some strength into the dough. Then let the dough sit for another 45 minutes.

4. Place plenty of rye flour on your table and turn out the dough onto the floured surface.

5. Keeping your hands well floured, shape the dough into a round ball and leave it for 15 minutes.

6. Form the ball of dough into a conical shape. (This will gradually flow during the final proof into a boule shape.)

7. Place the conical-shaped dough onto a baking paper–lined baking tray. Ideally, the tray should have no sides (or use a tray upside down). This will allow you to gently slide the fully risen boule (still on the baking paper) onto a hot baking stone within the oven.

8. Generously sprinkle dark rye flour over the surface of the dough.

9. Place a large plastic container upside down over the tray and dough. Leave to prove somewhere cool.

10. The dough is ready for baking when the top surface has the classic cracked appearance and has flowed sufficiently to look like a boule (but not flat, as this will indicate the dough has been left too long). This may only take 20 to 30 minutes. The cracking shows that the dough has expanded during this proving period.

11. Carefully slide the boule (still on the baking paper) onto a baking stone within the preheated oven and bake for 15 minutes at 480°F (250°C, or gas mark 10) and then reduce the oven temperature to 390°F (200°C, or gas mark 6) for approximately 45 minutes more. Make sure to remove the baking paper from the oven after approximately 25 minutes because, depending on the quality, it could disintegrate in the oven if left in for the entire hour.

12. Remove the baked boule from the oven and place on a cooling rack or use the common procedure for rye bread and wrap the boule in a tea towel and place into a lidded plastic container to cool. This helps the moisture inside to equilibrate around the loaf. If you can't wait that long, just go for it!

Yield: 1 large boule

TIP:

To contain the flow of the proving boule, you can place the conical of dough (step 7) into an 8-inch (20 cm) round cake pan greased with white vegetable shortening and then follow the rest of the steps.

FLOUR HYDRATION LEVEL (PERCENTAGE WATER TO FLOUR):

Recipe provides 89.5 percent hydration.

LITHUANIAN KEPTINIS CON SOPRACCIGLIO

I developed this bread with my local brewery, Pope's Yard. Keptinis is a Lithuanian *baked* beer where the malted barley is baked to give a much richer flavor to the beer. After baking some malted barley in my bread ovens for the brewery to use to make a batch of Keptinis beer, the smell was so good, I had to keep some to try and develop a bread containing it. This recipe is the resulting bread.

The baked malted barley porridge gives this bread a rich golden-brown color and a truly awesome malty flavor and aroma. You can also replace the dough water with a stout or porter (unless you are lucky enough to find some Keptinis beer locally). This will deliver a richer color and flavor to the baked bread.

BAKED MALTED BARLEY PORRIDGE:

400 g (14 ounces) crushed malted barley

600 g (1 pound 5¼ ounces) tap water (boiled)

1. Place the crushed malted barley into a bowl, pour in the hot water, and stir thoroughly.

2. Leave to soak for an hour.

3. Place the soaked, crushed malted barley into a small pan. The barley should be deeply piled in the pan.

4. Cover with foil, place in the preheated oven, and bake at 400°F (200°C, or gas mark 6).

5. It is ready when the internal temperature is over 194°F (90°C) and the top and bottom surface are well baked.

6. Leave in the pan to cool.

7. When cool enough to touch, remove the baked malted barley porridge from the roasting pan and place into a clean bowl. Stir to break up the porridge that has clumped together.

Note: You will end up with more baked malted barley porridge than the recipe requires. The excess can be stored in the fridge for up to 2 weeks to be used another time.

DOUGH:

440 g (15¹/₂ ounces) white bread flour, plus more for dusting

10 g (¹/₃ ounce) salt

170 g (6 ounces) wheat sour culture (100 percent hydration: fed twice daily for 3 days)

285 g (10 ounces) tap water

135 g (4³/₄ ounces) Baked Malted Barley Porridge

Ground rice or semolina, for dusting

1. Weigh the dry ingredients separately and place them into a large plastic bowl in the following order: flour first and then the salt.

2. Add the wheat sour culture and tap water and combine until a dough starts to form and the sides of the bowl are clean.

3. Remove the dough from the bowl and knead on a dry work surface until it becomes smooth and elastic, approximately 15 minutes.

Continues...

4. Use the windowpane test (see page 36) to check if the dough is fully developed.

5. Flatten the dough, spread the Baked Malted Barley Porridge on top, roll up, and then gently knead until thoroughly mixed together.

6. Divide the dough into two 500 g (1 pound 1½ ounce) pieces and gently shape into round balls.

7. Place the dough balls into a lidded plastic container and leave to bulk ferment for 30 minutes.

8. Remove the dough balls from the container and gently reshape.

9. Place back into the container for another 30 minutes.

10. Remove the dough balls from the container and once again gently reshape.

11. Place back into the container for another 30 minutes.

12. Remove the dough balls from the container. Form into cylindrical shapes and place upside down into your flour-dusted oblong proving baskets.

13. Place the proving baskets into a large, lidded plastic storage box and leave to fully prove. This could take from 3 to 6 hours, depending on the activity of the sour culture.

14. When fully proved, generously sprinkle some ground rice or semolina on a pizza peel or flat thin baking tray and turn out the dough from the proving basket onto the prepared surface.

15. Score the dough surface using a very sharp knife or lame (see page 40).

16. Slide the dough onto a baking stone or heavy baking tray in an oven preheated to 425°F (220°C, or gas mark 7) and steam the oven (see page 43).

17. Bake until golden brown, approximately 30 minutes.

18. Remove the baked loaves from the oven and place on a cooling rack.

Yield: 2 small loaves

FLOUR HYDRATION LEVEL (PERCENTAGE WATER TO FLOUR):

Recipe provides
70.5 percent hydration.

Increase water to 309 g
(11 ounces) to achieve
75 percent hydration.

Increase water to 335 g
(11³⁄₄ ounces) to achieve
80 percent hydration.

EDIBLE
AND POISONOUS
FLOWERS

Although flowers are colorful and fragrant, some are poisonous. If you are unsure of what the flower is, or whether it is edible, please do not use it. It's better to be safe than sorry.

My first attempt at making Botanical Bread used magnolia petals. Petals take longer to ferment than most other ingredients, and usually it is necessary to add some honey to help feed the yeasts. If you ferment flowers and fruit together, however, adding the supplemental honey may not be necessary.

WORDS OF WARNING

If you are going to use edible flowers in your botanical baking, there are important safety matters that you must be aware of and commit to memory before you begin.

Make sure you carefully and positively identify the variety you are using because many flowers are **poisonous**.

When searching for flowers to ferment, avoid picking faded, dusty, old, or diskolored flowers.

Avoid flowers close to a road or an area that animals use or frequent.

Do not use flowers that have been treated with pesticides.

Gently wash the flowers to remove any dirt or insects.

Only use the petals: diskard the stamens (the male reproductive parts), pistil (the female reproductive organ), and calyx (the outermost protective cover). The bitter "heel" at the base of the petal should also be removed.

EDIBLE FLOWERS

Here are some of the most popular and recognizable edible flowers used in foods.

EDIBLE FLOWERS THAT I RECOMMEND

Here is a list of edible flowers that I endorse, some of which I use frequently in my botanical baking with fantastic results!

ALPINE PINKS (*Dianthus*): Tasting of clove, these flowers are good in flavored sugars, oils, and vinegars.

CAMELLIA (*Camellia japonica*): These are used fresh as garnishes or dried for use in Asian cuisine.

CAPE JASMINE (*Gardenia jasminoides*): Extremely fragrant, this flower is ideal for pickling, preserving, and baking.

CORNFLOWER (*Centaurea cyanus*): This flower has a sweet and spicy clove-like flavor.

DAHLIA (*Dahlia pinnata*): Flavors of this flower range from water chestnut to spicy apple to carrot.

DANDELION (*Taraxacum officinale*): These flowers taste of honey when fresh.

FORGET-ME-NOT (*Myosotis sylvatica*): These flowers may be eaten on their own or used as a garnish.

FREESIA (*Freesia laxa*): This flower is great when infused in a tisane tea, or herbal tea, with lemon.

FRENCH MARIGOLD (*Tagetes patula*): This flower has spicy tarragon notes.

FUCHSIA (*Fuchsia magellanica*): You can enhance the flavor by removing any green and brown parts in addition to the stamen.

GLADIOLUS (*Gladiolus oppositiflorus*): These flowers are mild in taste, similar to lettuce.

HIBISCUS (*Hibiscus rosa-sinensis*): Add these to fruit salads or use to make a citrus-flavored tea.

HOLLYHOCK (*Alcea rosea*): You need to remove the center stamen and styles before eating. The petals can be crystallized and used for decoration.

HONEYSUCKLE (*Lonicera periclymenum*): Use the petals to make a syrup, pudding, or tea.

JASMINE: Only the species *Jasminum sambac* is edible; all other jasmine species are poisonous.

LAVENDER (*Lavandula angustifolia*): The purple flowers are best used in sweet dishes such as jams, jellies, scones, and biscuits.

LILAC (*Syringa vulgaris*): These flowers can be mixed with cream cheese or yogurt for a dip.

MAGNOLIA (*Magnolia*): The flowers can be pickled or used fresh in salads.

NASTURTIUM (*Nasturtium*): These flowers taste peppery, like watercress, and make an interesting salad addition as well as a flavorful pesto sauce.

PANSY (*Viola tricolor*): Mild and fresh-tasting, pansies can be used in a green salad or as a garnish.

PEONY (*Paeonia officinalis*): The petals work well in salads or can be lightly cooked and sweetened.

ROSE (*Rosa*): With their delicate fragrance, roses are widely used in drinks, fruit dishes, jams, and jellies. You can also crystallize the petals and use them to decorate cakes and other desserts.

SCENTED GERANIUMS (*Pelargonium graveolens*): The flavors range from citrus to nutmeg. The leaves and the petals are most often used to flavor baked goods such as cakes and liquids such as teas.

SUNFLOWER (*Helianthus*): The mild nutty taste makes the bright petals a colorful addition to salads.

VIOLET (*Viola*): An edible flower available in winter, violets are used to infuse flavor into jellies and liquids and can be candied and used to decorate desserts.

SOURCING INFORMATION ABOUT EDIBLE FLOWERS AND PLANTS

I cannot stress enough the importance of using a reputable source when searching out information about plants, flowers, and herbs used for human consumption.

One great source is the Royal Horticultural Society, the leading gardening charity in the UK, dedicated to advancing horticulture and promoting good gardening. For more information, you may visit their website at www.rhs.org.uk.

Here, I have included select information from their website of their suggestions and reasons for choosing certain edible flowers. I hope that this proves to be a helpful example of what to look for when it is time for you to begin researching what to use to ferment for your baking.

EDIBLE FLOWERS FROM YOUR GARDEN (COURTESY OF THE ROYAL HORTICULTURAL SOCIETY)

Homegrown flowers, free from pesticides and soiling by dogs and other pets, are best. Edible flowers are offered for sale but only use those labeled for *culinary purposes*, as these will have been grown in ways that ensure any pesticide residues are at a safe level or that they are pesticide-free. Store- or garden center-bought flowering plants should be grown on for at least three months to reduce the risk of pesticide residues and only the subsequent flowerings should be harvested. Many garden favorites are edible, and a few are listed below:

BERGAMOT (*Monardia didyma*): This flower has a strong spicy scent that makes good tea and complements bacon, poultry, rice, and pasta.

CHRYSANTHEMUM (*Chrysanthemum*): The petals add flavor and color to cream soups, fish chowder, and egg dishes in the same way as calendula (marigolds).

DAISY (*Bellis perennis*): They don't have a strong flavor, but the petals make an interesting garnish for cakes and salads.

DAY LILY (*Hemerocallis*): Add the buds and flowers to stir-fries, salads, and soups. They are crunchy with a peppery aftertaste, but they may have a laxative effect. Avoid buds damaged by gall midges.

ELDERFLOWER (*Sambucus nigra*): This flower is most often used to make wine and cordials. It can also be placed in a muslin bag to flavor tarts and jellies, but it must be removed before serving. Elderflowers can also be dipped in batter and deep-fried.

POT MARIGOLD (*Calendula officinalis*): This flower has an intense color and a peppery taste that is perfect in soups, stews, and desserts. The petals can be dried or pickled in vinegar or added to oil or butter.

PRIMROSE (*Primula vulgaris*): Crystallized or fresh primrose or cowslip flowers can be used to decorate cakes. They can also be frozen in ice cubes.

TIGER LILY (*Lilium leucanthemum* var. *tigrinum*): The delicate fragrance and flavor of this flower enhances salads, omelets, and poultry, plus it can be used as a stuffing for fish.

EDIBLE FLOWERS FROM YOUR VEGETABLE PATCH AND HERB GARDEN (COURTESY OF THE ROYAL HORTICULTURAL SOCIETY)

Herb flowers like basil, chives, lavender, mint, rosemary, and thyme impart a subtler flavor to food than the leaves. By adding sprigs of edible herb flowers like basil or marjoram to oils and butters, the delicate flavors can be used over a longer period. Some of these edible herb flowers are listed below:

BASIL (*Ocimum basilicum*): The sweet, clover-like flavor of this herb complements tomato dishes as well as oils, salad dressings, and soups. Use the aromatic leaves of both green and purple basil in Mediterranean dishes.

BORAGE (*Borago offincinalis*): The cucumber flavor of these attractive blue flowers adds interest to cakes, salads, and pâté. Flowers are easily removed and can be frozen in ice cubes or crystallized.

CHIVES (*Allium schoenoprasum*): With a mild onion flavor, chives are good in salads, egg dishes, and sauces for fish.

CLOVER (*Trifolium pratense*): Both red and white clover flowers can be used to garnish fruit and green salads, or wine can be made from whole red flowers.

COURGETTE OR MARROW FLOWERS (*Cucurbita*): These can be eaten hot in a tomato sauce or cold and stuffed with cooked rice, cheese, nuts, or meat. Use male flowers so as not to reduce yield.

DILL (*Anethum graveolens*): With an aniseed flavor, dill is an ideal addition to salads, vegetables, and fish dishes. Add the flowers to mayonnaise, white sauce, and pickles.

FENNEL (*Foeniculum vulgare*): All parts are edible and enhance salmon, pâtés, and salads. Flowers preserved in oil or vinegar can be used in winter.

GARDEN PEA (*Pisum sativum*): Add flowers and young shoots to salad for a fresh pea taste.

MINT (*Mentha* spp): Apple, pineapple, and ginger mint, plus peppermint and spearmint flowers, can all be used in oil, vinegar, and butter for both sweet and savory dishes.

ROSEMARY (*Rosmarinus officinalis*): The sweet flavor of rosemary leaves can be used fresh to garnish salads and tomato dishes or to flavor butter or oil.

SALAD ROCKET (*Eruca vescaria*): This adds a sharp flavor to salads or can be preserved in oil or butter to accompany meat.

Another great resource for information about all thing plants is the United States Department of Agriculture (USDA) website: Fact Sheets and Plant Guides. You can visit them at www.plants.usda.gov/java/factSheet.

POISONOUS FLOWERS

Here is a list of common flowers that are poisonous. This list is **by no means extensive**, so always check with a trustworthy source (such as those mentioned above) before using any vegetation for fermenting.

BLEEDING HEART (*Lamprocapnos spectabilis*): Consumption will cause vomiting, diarrhea, and tremors.

BLUEBELL (*Hyacinthoides*): This flower contains toxic glycosides.

CALLA LILY (*Zantedeschia*): Consumption will cause drooling, vomiting, and oral pain.

CLEMATIS (*Clematis occidentalis*): Contact can cause skin irritation; consumption will cause severe mouth pain.

DAFFODIL (*Narcissus*): Consumption will cause vomiting, diarrhea, burning, and irritation due to the toxin lycorine.

FOXGLOVE (*Digitalis*): This flower contains poisons that will cause drooling, vomiting, seizures, dilated pupils, and even death.

GYPSOPHILA (*Gypsophila paniculata*): Contact can cause skin irritation; consumption will cause vomiting and diarrhea.

HYDRANGEA (*Hydrangea macrophylla*): This flower contains a small amount of cyanide and consumption can cause vomiting, fever, and diarrhea.

IRIS (*Iris germanica*): Consumption will cause vomiting, fever, and diarrhea.

LARKSPUR (*Delphinium*): Its toxic alkaloids are fast-acting and potentially life-threatening.

LILY-OF-THE-VALLEY (*Convallaria majalis*): Consumption will cause vomiting, diarrhea, and seizures.

MORNING GLORY (*Ipomoea*): Consumption will cause diarrhea, vomiting, and hallucinations.

OLEANDER (*Ipomoea purpurea*): The whole plant is highly toxic and is one of the most toxic garden plants.

POPPY (*Papaveraceae*): All poppies are poisonous.

RHODODENDRON (*Rhododendron ferrugineum*): Its toxins can have a negative impact on heart rhythm and blood pressure.

TULIP (*Tulipa*): Consumption will cause vomiting, diarrhea, and drooling.

PROTEOLYTIC ENZYME-CONTAINING FOODS

Fruits like papaya (papain), kiwi (actinidain), pineapple (bromelain), and figs (ficain) all contain proteolytic enzymes (proteases). In dough, the gluten is formed from protein in the flour, but these proteins break down in the presence of protease, creating a weak dough structure. These fruits all contain different levels of proteolytic enzymes and therefore can cause varying amounts of damage to the dough. One of my favorite botanical breads I make is the Fig and Fennel Farmhouse Loaf. I have never noticed any detrimental effect coming from the fermented fig or the added soft ready-to-eat figs in the dough. In contrast, the papain found in papaya is strong enough to be used as a meat tenderizer, so it is therefore best avoided when preparing bread.

GLOSSARY

BAKING STONE
Also called a pizza stone, this is a thick piece of stoneware used in the oven to increase the heat and help form a crispy crust on the bottom of a loaf of bread or a pizza.

BANNETON
Also called a proofing basket or cane basket, this is a type of basket used to provide structure for shaped loaves of bread during proving, or proofing. A banneton is normally used for doughs that are too wet or soft to maintain their shape during the rising process.

BIGA
The Italian term for a preferment, which is a portion of salt-free bread dough that is made up to twenty-four hours in advance and then incorporated into the final recipe.

BLOOMER BREAD
Also called London Bloomer Bread, this is a crusty loaf of bread with rounded ends and several parallel diagonal slashes across the top.

BOULE
Comes from the French word for *ball* and refers to the traditional shape for a loaf of French bread that resembles a squashed ball.

BOWL SCRAPER
A kitchen tool made of flexible plastic that is used to remove the contents of a mixing bowl or jar.

BRAMLEY APPLES
Bramley apples are a traditional British cooking apple. Granny Smith apples are an acceptable substitute to attain similar results.

CASTER SUGAR
A super-fine granulated sugar.

DEMERARA SUGAR
A variety of raw cane sugar that has a large grain, a crunchy texture, and is pale brown in color.

FARMHOUSE LOAF PAN
A rectangular bread pan with rounded corners used to make a flour-topped, softly baked loaf.

FEATHERING
To decorate by *feathering* is simply to draw, or pipe, lines of icing across an already iced background in a feather or fan design.

KILNER JARS
Kilner jars are glass jars used for preserving and bottling food that were first produced by John Kilner and Co., in Yorkshire, England. The original jars were rubber-sealed, screw-topped jars, but the company now manufactures a variety of sizes and shapes, as well as their famous Clip Top Storage Jars that have a clamp-down lid rather than a screwed-on lid.

LAME
A kitchen tool comprised of a double-sided blade on a long handle that is used to slash, or score, the tops of bread loaves just before the bread is placed in the oven.

LICORICE STICK
The dried root of the *Glycyrrhiza glabra* plant. It is used in cooking to sweeten candy and beverages and is also recognized for its medicinal benefits.

MADAGASCAR VANILLA
Also called Bourbon vanilla, this is a flavoring derived from orchids that is produced in Madagascar and the neighboring islands in the southwestern Indian Ocean and in Indonesia.

MIXED SPICE
A British spice blend that includes a balance of some or all of the following ground spices: cinnamon, coriander seed, caraway, nutmeg, ginger, cloves, allspice, and mace.

OVEN SPRING
The final burst of rising after the proved dough is placed in the oven, before the crust starts to form.

PALLET KNIFE
Also called an offset spatula, this is a kitchen utensil designed especially for spreading a substance onto a flat surface, such as icing on a bun.

PÂTE FERMENTÉE
A prefermentation method where a portion of fermented dough is reserved and stored for use in a future recipe.

PEEL

A *peel*, also called a *baker's peel* or *pizza peel*, is a baker's tool used to slide loaves of bread, pizzas, and other baked goods in and out of the oven. Resembling a shovel, they are generally made of wood, but can also have a carrying surface (the *blade* of the shovel) made of metal with an attached wood handle.

POOLISH

Like a *biga*, this is a type of preferment that is prepared separately the day before, but it contains salt and a higher percentage of liquid than a biga and is more like a batter.

POURED FONDANT ICING

A sweet, creamy paste used as an icing or frosting or for making candies. This is not the same as *rolled fondant* that contains gelatin and is rolled out into sheets used for cake decorating, giving a smooth look.

RETARDING

Retarding dough is the process of placing the dough in the refrigerator for a lengthened fermenting or proofing period.

SAVARIN PAN/ BABA PAN

A large ring-shaped cake pan or mold that has a hole in the center. A *rum baba pan* is a cork-shaped pan with no hole.

SCRAPER

A *bench scraper* or *dough scraper* is a rigid kitchen tool used by bakers to manipulate dough or to scrape cutting boards. They are traditionally metal with a wooden handle, but can also be made from plastic.

SICILIAN LEMONS

Sicilian lemons, or Siracusa lemons, are lemons that are grown in Sicily, Italy, and are prized for their abundance of juice and strong essential oils. The most popular variety is called *femminello*.

SLAP-AND-FOLD METHOD

A method of working with, or kneading, dough, also called the French fold. The steps are as follows:

Mix all the ingredients, ensuring that there are no dry lumps of flour, and flip the dough onto an unfloured surface.

Use both hands to grasp the dough, placing your fingers under the dough and your thumbs above it.

Lift up the dough and flip it over.

Then, grasp the end of the dough and stretch it toward yourself.

Fold the stretched piece of dough over on itself.

Repeat until the desired consistency is achieved.

SPLIT TIN LOAF (BREAD)

This is a British term for a basic white bread dough, or sandwich bread, that is baked in a loaf pan and has a deep slash across the top.

STEAM THE OVEN

The technique of adding steam to your home oven by one of several methods (such as with a pan of water or by spritzing the oven). This method is used to increase dough oven spring and to enhance crust color and crispness.

STRETCH-AND-FOLD METHOD

A method of working with, or kneading, dough. The steps are as follows:

Mix all the ingredients, ensuring that there are no dry lumps of flour. The dough can be worked in its container or on a clean surface.

Pull the dough from one side and stretch it vertically.

Then, fold the stretched piece over the remainder of the dough.

Repeat this routine for each side of the dough, working in a circular manner.

Repeat until the desired consistency is achieved.

Optionally, the dough can be flipped over any time during this process.

STRONG FLOUR

Strong flour, also called bread flour, is flour with a very high gluten-forming protein content (13 to 14 percent).

WINDOWPANE TEST

This is a method for testing if dough is fully kneaded. The steps are as follows:

Take a small piece of dough, roll it into a ball, and let it rest for a minute.

Flatten the dough with your fingers and, grasping it between both your thumbs and first two fingers, gently spread the dough apart.

If the dough is completely kneaded, it should stretch, without tearing or breaking, into a thin membrane that you can see your fingers through.

AUTHOR BIO

PAUL BARKER, THE BOTANICAL BAKER

With over thirty-five years of experience in his field, Paul Barker has been described as a trailblazer in the baking industry. A qualified baker, pâtissier, chocolatier, cake decorator, and flour miller, he has worked in both the craft and the scientific aspects of baking.

In 2005, Paul and his wife Tricia set up their Bakery and Training Centre, Cinnamon Square. Since opening, Cinnamon Square has gone from strength to strength, winning accolades along the way. On a personal level, Paul has won the Skills Achievement Award, the Product Innovation Award from the British Baking Industry twice, and has been a finalist for Best Tutor for two years running in the Cookery School Awards. Paul's breads have won many awards, including Great Taste Awards, World Bread Awards, and Baking Industry Awards.

Paul is a passionate baker with an infectious enthusiasm for his craft. He spends much of his time pioneering and developing new products for the bakery and teaching adults and children to bake. He taught over 17,000 children in Cinnamon Square's first fifteen years.

Paul was an advisor setting up BBC's *The Great British Bake Off*, he has written many baking articles and recipes; he is a regular guest on BBC radio; and he has appeared on the *Good Food Show* and *Britain's Best Bakery* as well as filming baking tutorials for Videojug.

Paul's first book, *Cinnamon Square: A Measured Approach*, is a unique recipe book focusing on using precision measurement and techniques to help home bakers achieve consistency and greater confidence in their baking.

ACKNOWLEDGMENTS

I first would like to thank my wife Tricia, the rock of the Barker family, for all her support over many years with my passion for baking, which borders on obsession! Without her, I certainly would not be the person I am today.

The second person I owe a debt of gratitude to is my late father Ted. He allowed me the freedom to make my own path in life, supporting me whenever the need arose. Dad installed many great values in me that I continue use in my personal and work life. He was proud of all my achievements and was "tickety boo" to learn that this book was to be published. Unfortunately Dad passed away before the book was completed, so his memory will forever carry on within these words.

I would like to dedicate this book to you, Dad.

I also would like to thank Jonathan Simcosky and the team at Quarry Books for investing time to fully appreciate the rationale behind my *Naturally Fermented Bread* idea and for their commitment to evolve the idea into this beautifully presented book. Considering we reside on different continents, I think a fantastic result has been achieved. And finally, big thanks go to Joanna Goode for her stunning photography.

Paul

INDEX